ACKNOWLEDGMENTS

Special thanks to some of my most important "teachers":

John LaPorta, Jack Petersen, Herb Pomeroy, Bill Leavitt, Carl Shroeder, Abe Laboriel, Gary Burton, Steve Swallow, Jeff Berlin, Jerry Bergonzi, and Gary Chaffee.

And finally, special thanks to Liz Hamill, who typed, edited, did the manuscript, suggested, questioned, encouraged, learned, taught, and laughed a lot. Without her immense help (in seemingly all directions at once), I could never have written this book.

the advancing guitarist

APPLYING GUITAR CONCEPTS & TECHNIQUES

by MICK GOODRICK

This book is dedicated to Pat,
partially because he made it possible,
but mostly because he never needed it.

Produced by John Cerullo
Art Direction by John Flannery
Text Edited by Rick Mattingly
Music Edited by Jefferson Newman

ISBN 978-0-88188-589-7

INTRODUCTION

This is a do-it-yourself book. It's not a method book. You supply the method; you do it yourself. I may make some suggestions along the way — point out some things that seem important or relevant. But what you do with it is entirely your own business; it's totally up to you. Don't depend on anyone but yourself for your own musical growth. (I've taken steps to arrange this book so that you *have* to depend on yourself as much as possible.)

This isn't to say that you can't or shouldn't learn from others. In music, you have to. However, I can't stress enough the importance of being self-reliant and self-motivated. The material presented in this book could keep anyone very busy for at least several lifetimes, in my opinion. In all honesty, I must admit that I feel I've only just begun to scratch the surface of what's presented here. (And that's after playing for 28 years and teaching for 23.) So don't assume that I know all of this and you have to learn as much as I know. (Don't assume anything!) Take what you need — what you can use. When you've had enough, put it away for a while. Come back when you're ready.

By itself, a book has absolutely no value; it's a dead thing. But in conjunction with a living human being who can understand, work, and grow, a book can be very useful. I'm saying that *you* are what's valuable, not the book. I've taken the time to supply the book. You take the time to supply *you*. Then we'll both be happy. Guaranteed!

Best wishes,
Mick Goodrick

CONTENTS

III. COMMENTARIES

I. THE APPROACH

Introduction to Fingerboard Mechanics

Your ability to play music on the guitar depends to a large extent on how well you know the instrument. Most guitarists have never had a chance to learn the instrument in an intelligent, logical and complete manner. The fact is that the vast majority of guitar method books don't really explain very much at all, and the vast majority of guitar teachers are the products of these methods. As a general rule, guitar methods don't concern themselves with helping you to increase your overall comprehension of the instrument. Guitar methods get you to *do* a lot of things (which certainly can be useful). They show you a method of how to do something. But these methods seldom, if ever, lead to a growth of your understanding of how things work on the instrument. If anything, they lead to a narrowing of possibilities because you don't have to figure out very much by yourself. You just have to follow instructions. When you know the method, you are the result of the method. If you teach, you tend to teach the method (perhaps with a few modifications — a few improvements). The method can actually become more important than the music it is supposed to help facilitate. This is not so good.

All of the above helps to explain why this present volume is not a method book. No methods are given. Methods may be implied or hinted at, but only in a very loose way. Methods may be deduced by the reader (in fact, *need* to be deduced), but the results of the readers' pursuing such methods are totally based on individual intelligence, present knowledge, interest, and creativity.

What I'm trying to do is present information and facts. You will draw from this information exactly what you are able to draw, based on current understanding. This way, you get just what you are capable of; what you deserve; what you need.

> Two glasses of different sizes sit on a table.
> From the standpoint of their function as glasses, the
> important thing is not whether one is larger or smaller,
> but rather that both are full.

Fingerboard Mechanics

First Thing to Learn: Up and Down a String (Single String Playing)

Second Thing to Learn: Across the Neck and Back (Position Playing)

Third Thing to Learn: Combine All of Both Previous Possibilities (Combination Playing or "The Realm of the Electric Ice-Skating Rink").

If I were a real tough disciplinarian, I would have ended this lesson one sentence ago. But this "area" is so crucially important, so misunderstood and so seldom mentioned at all, that I really have to go into a little bit of depth on this.

Any guitarist who has played at all seriously knows that position playing is very important. Also, position playing is a huge project. Lots of stuff to learn. Years of work involved. I think we can agree on this point (more on position playing follows later).

The point that I'm trying to make (which may be one of the most important points in this book) is that position playing is not even half of it. (Probably not even a third of it!) Equally as important as position playing is playing up and down one string. I'd even go so far as to say that it's more important than position playing just because it's so seldom explored. In addition, I might add that standardized methods for position playing have been in existence for some time, whereas methods for playing up and down one string are practically non-existent, at least in the WEST.

It boils down to this: a lot of guitarists today know about position playing, but very few know about playing up and down one string. Not surprisingly (at least to me) some of those few who do know are among the very best guitarists on the planet these days. (Please, no names!)

In most guitar method books, no mention is ever made of playing up and down one string. This omission is a huge oversight, because playing on a single string is absolutely the most logical place to begin on a guitar. Consider the following observations:

- The simplest way to see notes is in a straight line.
- A single string *is* a straight line.
- On a single string, there is a direct relationship between interval distance and movement in space.
- Playing on a single string helps to eliminate two potential problems: "paralysis" (fear of movement) and "acrophobia" (fear of higher frets), since the entire length of the fingerboard is utilized from the very beginning.
- This approach is conducive to learning note locations because you can't rely on a fingering pattern (as in position playing).
- The problem of changing strings is eliminated. This simplifies the right-hand function and displays the principles of left hand function in their purest form.
- Different types of phrasing and articulations can be played very consistently.
- Elements of fundamental theory can be shown to a beginner in clear and simple visual and aural terms:
  Intervals, scale construction, chords, arpeggios, etc. The same could be said for dynamics, articulations, and timbre.
- Someone probably invented a one-stringed instrument (let's call it a unitar!) long before anyone ever thought of two strings, let alone six of them. So it would seem sensible to learn in the same way that the instrument developed chronologically.
- Many stringed instruments in Eastern countries are played in a much more "up and down the neck" fashion (most notably, the sitar). Do you have any idea how long the music of India has been around?

All of the above contribute to support my personal contention that you have no real understanding of the fingerboard until you've spent a lot of time playing up and down the strings individually. If all you know is position playing, you can't even begin to see the whole fingerboard. In fact, you can't even understand the proper uses and advantages of position playing until you've played up and down on the strings a lot.

The strange thing about all of this is that it's really so obvious. (Hidden in the Eye of the Sun, so to speak.) One can't help but wonder how it is that hardly anyone has noticed it.

It is safe to say that you would do well to spend some time playing on one string. Doing this (in itself) would begin to completely transform your understanding of the fingerboard within two or three weeks. I could almost guarantee it. Consequently, the approach that this volume presents goes like this:

1. Playing up and down each of the six strings individually (The Science of the Unitar)
2. Playing up and down five combinations of two adjacent strings (Moveable Mini positions)
3. Study of Intervals: Melodic and Harmonic ("Poor Man's Guide to Counterpoint")
4. The Open Position
5. Position Playing
6. Combination Playing ("The Realm of the Electric Ice-Skating Rink")

Playing Up and Down a Single String (The Science of the Unitar)

Three Principles of Left-Hand Movement:

1. **Groupings** (two, three, or four notes based on what the left hand can cover)
2. **Hand-carries or shifts** (moving to a higher pitched note with lower numerical finger; moving to lower pitched note with higher numerical finger; linking two or more different groupings)
3. **Slides** (using the same finger to play different consecutive pitches — no glissandi)

Breakdown of Finger Possibilities:

a. Four possibilities of one finger at a time

1. 1st finger
2. 2nd finger
3. 3rd finger
4. 4th finger

No groupings, no shifts, all slides

b. Six possibilities of two fingers at a time

1. 1 and 2
2. 1 and 3
3. 1 and 4
4. 2 and 3
5. 2 and 4
6. 3 and 4

Two note groupings, shifts, slides

c. Four possibilites of three fingers at a time

1. 1, 2, 3
2. 1, 2, 4
3. 1, 3, 4
4. 2, 3, 4

Two and three note groupings, shifts, slides

d. All four fingers: combine all previous possibilities two, three , and four note groupings, shifts, slides

Why would you play up and down one string with only one finger? Because you'd learn things that can't be learned any other way. This type of approach is what I call "disadvantage exercises". By deliberately working within the confine of a particular limitation (i.e., only one finger or two or three), we can learn much. Some people might ask, "Why bother playing with only one finger when you've got four? You can't play much with one finger anyway!" But the question is really, "How much can you play with one finger and what could you learn?" When playing with only one finger, do you rely on fingering patterns or note locations? Is there any conceivable use for a technique whereby you cannot play what you normally play?

How much should you play up and down one string? (Good question!) How do you expect me to know how much you should play up and down one string? (Another good question!)

Actually, I guess you should play up and down own string as much as you need to play. (I'm really being a great help, aren't I?) When you seem to reach your own saturation point, stop for a while. Do something else. You can always come back to playing up and down one string. When you come back to it, you'll more than likely see some things about it that you didn't see the first time. A lot of things in music are like that. Probably all of them.

Does it make sense to have East and West without North and South?
Does it make sense to have longitude without latitude?
Does it make sense to have horizontal without vertical?
Does it make sense to have position playing without playing up and down one string?
Should I be ashamed at having to ask such silly questions?

Activities — Application

1. Map out all natural notes (A, B, C, D, E, F, G) up and down each of the six strings individually. (Entire length of the fingerboard.)

2. Record suggested modal vamps on your tape recorder. Each modal vamp should be at least two but not more than four minutes in length. This way, all seven vamps should fit on one side of tape (30 minutes).

3. Play back the tape from the beginning, while improvising melodies against each modal vamp, but using only one string. Seven modes on six strings makes 42 possibilities. Two obvious approaches come to mind:

   A. Play one string through all seven modal vamps; repeat same procedure five times using the other strings, one at a time.

   B. Play through one modal vamp six times, once for each string. Repeat same procedure six times using each of the other modal vamps.

   One less obvious choice comes to mind:

   C. Write each of the 42 possibilities on a fairly large piece of paper (8 1/2 x 11). With scissors, cut out each one. (You'll then have 42 small pieces of paper.) Place them all in some kind of small container. Mix them up. Pull out one piece of paper at random and play what it says (i.e., E phrygian, B string). Repeat 41 times as desired.

It's probably a good idea to try each of these three approaches at some point. But, for the present, just pick whichever one seems most sensible to you right now. Later on, try either or both of the other two possibilities.

Temporary Rules:

1. Don't use any bends larger than a half step. You can only bend:

   1. B → C
   2. E → F
   3. C → B
   4. F → E

2. Don't play the following notes: C# D# F# G# A# Db Eb Gb Ab Bb

   For our purposes, they are wrong. No exceptions.

3. Don't change strings. If you're soloing against G Mixolydian on the low E string, stay there. Be patient. Don't jump to another string just because you start to get bored or repetitive in your soloing. Maybe play less for a while, or maybe more. Or maybe softer, or maybe louder. (They don't call it improvising for nothin' you know!) But stay on that one string. For the time being, that one string is your entire instrument, your entire musical voice. (You *really* should listen to some good sitar music!)

Observations:

1. Here are some things that you can do on one string that a piano player can't do at all:

   a. vibrato

   b. bending (remember, only half steps: B-C; E-F)

   c. hammer-ons/pull-offs

   d. glissandi

   e. harmonics (natural notes only)

   f. muffle the string

   g. change the tone quality by attacking the string in a different place.

   Make sure you experiment with all of them.

2. Each mode has its own mood. (What sort of mode are you in today?)

3. The half steps in each mode are very important. Let's look at them:

	E-F	**F-E**	**B-C**	**C-B**
Ionian:	3-4	4-3	7-8	8-7
Dorian:	2-b3	b3-2	6-b7	b7-6
Phrygian:	1-b2	b2-1	5-b6	b6-5
Lydian:	7-8	8-7	#4-5	5-#4
Mixolydian:	6-b7	b7-6	3-4	4-3
Aeolian:	5-b6	b6-5	2-b3	b3-2
Locrian:	4-b5	b5-4	1-b2	b2-1

   These half steps contain the problem areas of each mode, or the places where you can run into trouble with unwanted dissonance. However, the half steps also contain the individual color characteristics of each mode. So, both aspects taken into consideration, you really need to understand how half steps work.

4. Two very important ways of thinking about modes are:

   a.derivative: D Dorian is C major scale starting on the second degree (finding the major scale from which the mode is derived)

   b.parallel: D Dorian is D major scale with b3 and b7 (constructing the mode from a *parallel* major scale/same root)

   Since we are using the modes of C major scale, it would seem that our approach is derivative. However, when you are playing against a vamp, I'd encourage you to think of the mode from the root of the tonic chord (parallel). We'll discuss this in more detail later on.

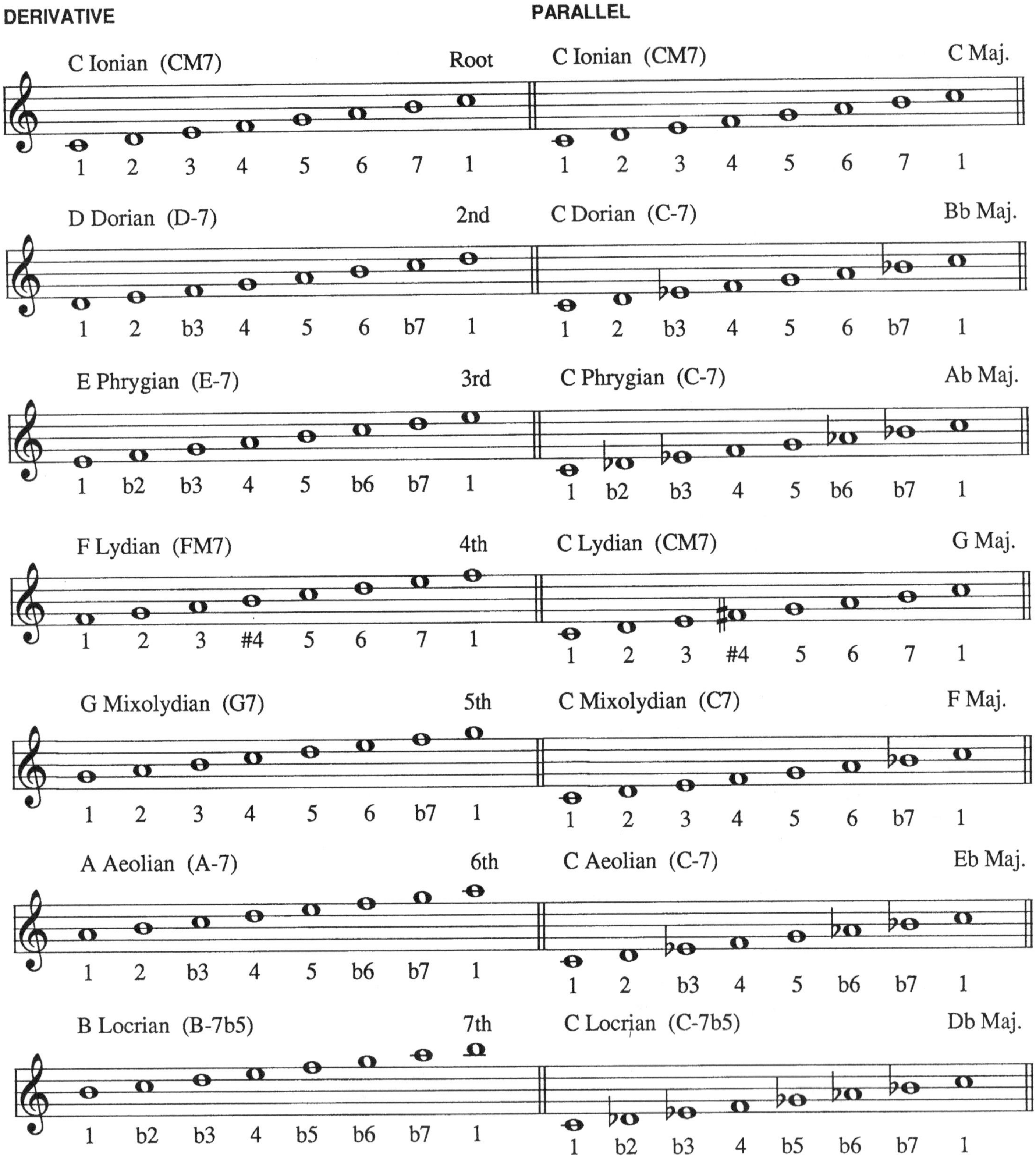
DERIVATIVE
PARALLEL
C Ionian (CM7) Root
1 2 3 4 5 6 7 1
C Ionian (CM7) C Maj.
1 2 3 4 5 6 7 1
D Dorian (D-7) 2nd
1 2 b3 4 5 6 b7 1
C Dorian (C-7) Bb Maj.
1 2 b3 4 5 6 b7 1
E Phrygian (E-7) 3rd
1 b2 b3 4 5 b6 b7 1
C Phrygian (C-7) Ab Maj.
1 b2 b3 4 5 b6 b7 1
F Lydian (FM7) 4th
1 2 3 #4 5 6 7 1
C Lydian (CM7) G Maj.
1 2 3 #4 5 6 7 1
G Mixolydian (G7) 5th
1 2 3 4 5 6 b7 1
C Mixolydian (C7) F Maj.
1 2 3 4 5 6 b7 1
A Aeolian (A-7) 6th
1 2 b3 4 5 b6 b7 1
C Aeolian (C-7) Eb Maj.
1 2 b3 4 5 b6 b7 1
B Locrian (B-7b5) 7th
1 b2 b3 4 b5 b6 b7 1
C Locrian (C-7b5) Db Maj.
1 b2 b3 4 b5 b6 b7 1

Arranged in order of brightness:

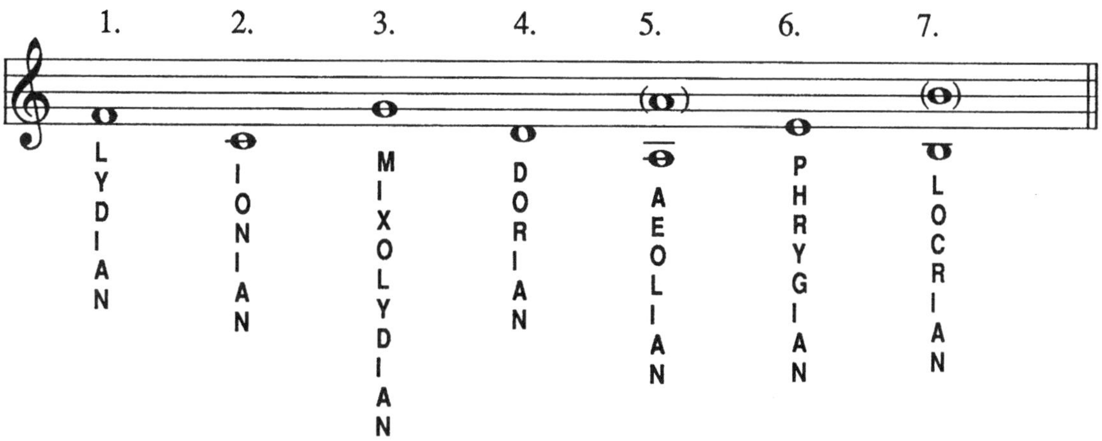
1.
2.
3.
4.
5.
6.
7.
LYDIAN
IONIAN
MIXOLYDIAN
DORIAN
AEOLIAN
PHRYGIAN
LOCRIAN

Arranged in order of brightness:

1. Lydian: #4
2. Ionian: 0
3. Mixolydian: b7
4. Dorian: b7, b3, (b3, b7)
5. Aeolian: b7, b3, b6 (b3, b6, b7)
6. Phrygian: b7, b3, b6, b2 (b2, b3, b6, b7)
7. Locrian: b7, b3, b6, b2, b5 (b2, b3, b5, b6, b7)

C Ionian

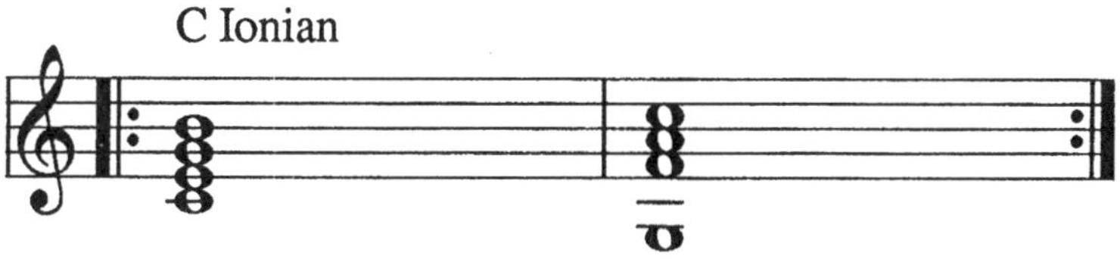

D Dorian

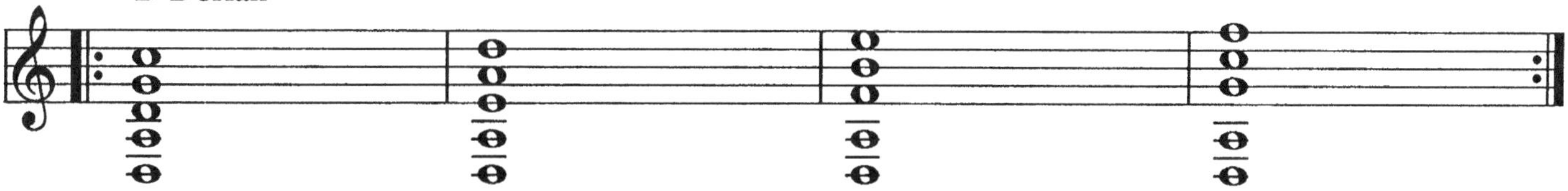

E Phyrgian

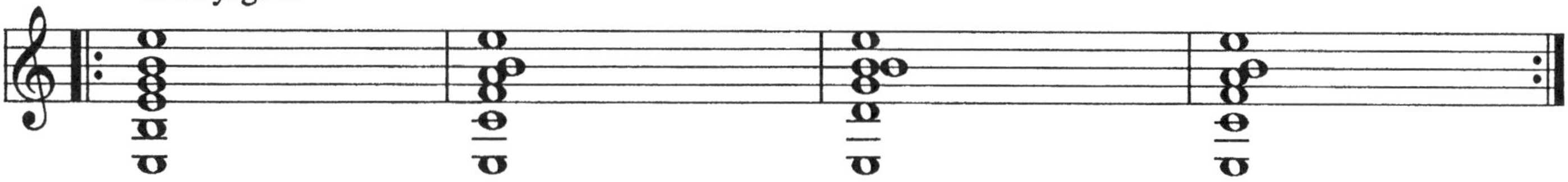

F Lydian

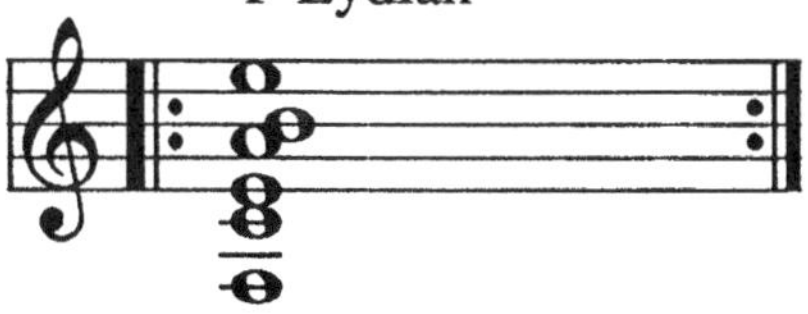

Can be arpeggiated for interest.

G Mixolydian

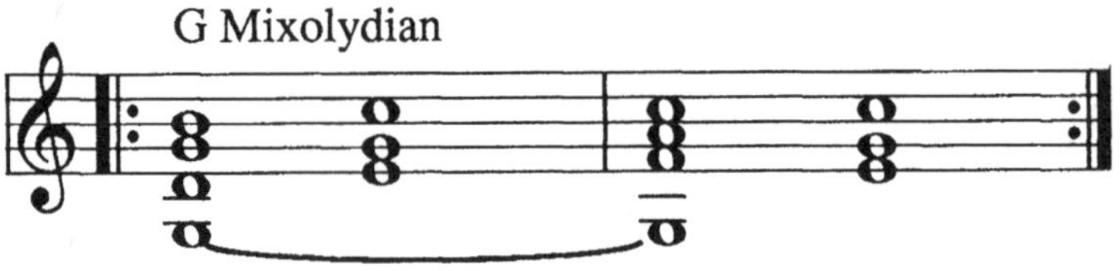

A Aoelian

B Locrian

Modes; Chord-Scales: I

Modes and chord-scales are extremely important. I think any serious improvising guitarist would be wise to become as familiar as possible with them. Although it's true that many fine players are not especially knowledgeable about modes, this is definitely the exception, not the rule. (And it's going to become more so as time goes on.) However, I might also point out that there are many guitarists who know a lot about modes and still don't play very well. So let's not start to equate modal knowledge with playing ability or musicality. Let's just say that modes are real important.

Modes provide an excellent overview of melodic and harmonic possibilities. (Modal thinking is both melodic and harmonic simultaneously: G7 alt. is equally a scale with infinite melodic possibilities as well as a chord-type with vast harmonic possibilities.) Keep in mind that all of this amounts to a lifelong study. There is no end to how much you could learn about modes and their implications.

It seems that the kind of problems that many guitarists have with modes are twofold. First of all, the very nature of modes includes so much within it that the overview aspect can sometimes lead to confusion instead of clarification (not seeing the trees for the forest). Secondly, the complicated nature of the guitar tends to lend itself to very incomplete understanding, laden with gaps. I think these problems can be overcome and/or worked through by an intelligent and thorough approach to both learning the materials and learning the instrument.

Playing on Two Adjacent Strings: Moveable Mini-positions

We have five sets of two adjacent strings:

E and A	(Perfect 4th)
A and D	(Perfect 4th)
D and G	(Perfect 4th)
G and B	(Major 3rd)
B and E	(Perfect 4th)

Notice that four of the five sets involve the interval of a perfect 4th. The other one (G and B) involves a major 3rd. This means that all groupings of notes will be different on this set. This does complicate things a little, but it also provides unique possibilities that wouldn't occur otherwise.

So now you get to improvise on seven modal vamps with five sets of two adjacent strings. That's 35 possibilities altogether. You'll find that this approach gives you the advantages of playing up and down two single strings, plus the advantages of partial position playing simultaneously. You can play a lot of things on two adjacent strings! Melodic leaps of 4ths, 5ths, and 6ths are much easier now than before (on one string). You'll find five or six notes under your fingers in one area instead of two or three as before. (Thus the term: Movable mini-positions.)

This is also an opportunity to make a detailed study of the right-hand picking techniques that involve movement between two adjacent strings. Work with this a lot; it's extremely important.

Use the same modal vamps to begin with. However, before too long, you might want to change the vamps. You may see the need to explore other tempos and/or time feels. Also, you might see the necessity of figuring out some higher register vamps for soloing on the lower sets of two adjacent strings to avoid the "muddiness" that could occur when low-register bass notes in the original version of the vamps clash with low register melody notes (i.e., on E and A strings).

So, go ahead and figure out some new vamps for the seven modes. Just remember: use all seven notes in each vamp and try to establish a clear sense at the root. Don't use sharps or flats. (Improvising vamps is something you need to be able to do a lot of the time anyway.)

When you're soloing, you might experiment with using only three fingers, or only two fingers, or even only one finger as was indicated in the previous section on playing up and down a single string. Since you now have two strings to play with, the effect of omitting one or two or three left-hand fingers will be very different.

Playing on two adjacent strings is the point where "patterns" really start to emerge from the fingerboard. And that's great; it's a very important aspect of the guitar. But also keep in mind the importance of knowing the *names* of the notes as well as the importance of knowing the *function* of the notes relative to the root of the particular mode you're playing on.

You'll probably find yourself playing more notes now than you did before (on a simgle string). And that's okay. Sometimes, it's a lot of fun to play a lot of notes. But don't get completely lost in a lot of notes. (At least, not for too long!) *Be musical.* That's something that merits being remembered.

Study of Intervals: Melodic and Harmonic (Poor Man's Guide to Counterpoint)

As guitarists, we tend to think either "lead" or "rhythm"; either "solo" or "comping"; either "melody" or "chords." (Melody could be defined as different notes in succession; harmony as different notes simultaneously.) In the early stages, melodies are "licks"; chords are "grips". We tend to think of these two important areas of music in very different ways. (Part of which is understandable; there are differences.) But are melody and harmony really all that different? We'll see.

Here's a very simple way to look at it: melody has to do with playing one note at a time. Harmony has to do with playing three, four, five or six notes at a time. The usual way to begin the study of harmony involves triads (three notes at a time); this is usually followed by 7th chords (four notes at a time); then 9th, 11th and 13th chords (five, six and seven notes at a time). The questions remains: "What about two notes at a time?"

The study of two notes at a time would be called the study of intervals. The musical discipline that deals with intervals is counterpoint. Counterpoint means point against point (which could be note against note). Counterpoint also means melody against melody. The point against point angle is vertical. The melody against melody angle is horizontal.

The notes C and E are a major third apart. Play C, then E: that's melody. Play C and E simultaneously: That's the beginning of harmony. You can't call it a chord. (It's a C chord; no, it's A minor; no, it's F Major 7th; no, it's F#7 alt.; no, it's Ab+M7; no it's Bb lydian, etc., etc.) It could be a lot of things. But what it *is* is a major third.

Counterpoint can be viewed as the study of intervals that helps to dissolve rigid ways of thinking about melody as one thing and harmony as another. (Melodies have harmonic implications; chords and chord progressions have melodic implications.)

So to review:

Melody	**Counterpoint**	**Harmony**
One note at a time	Study of intervals two notes at a time (Also, two melodies at a time	Three notes at a time (triads) four notes at a time (7th chords) five, six, seven notes at a time (9th, 11th, 13th chords)

Now, thinking about what an arpeggio is (slight digression):
Arpeggio — like a "melted" chord
Chord — like a "frozen" arpeggio

Counterpoint (or the study of intervals) is one of the most neglected and important aspects of the guitar. It is the other "area" of work on the guitar that most guitarists are both deficient in as well as in need of. (The first "area" was playing up and down one string, as you'll no doubt recall!) You'd do well to work hard at this "area". You'll never regret it.

A. Four Types of Contrapuntal Motion:

Parallel: both voices move the same distance in the same direction.

Similar: both voices move different distances in the same direction.

Contrary: each voice moves any distance in the opposite direction.

Oblique: one voice moves while the other stays where it is.

Parallel

Similar

Contrary

Oblique

Intervals to work with for now:

2nds: minor 2nd (half step)
major 2nd (whole step)

3rds: minor 3rd (step and a half: 3 half steps)
major 3rd (2 whole steps: 4 half steps)

4ths: perfect 4th (2 1/2 steps: 5 half steps)
augmented 4th (3 whole steps: 6 half steps: the octave in half)

5ths: diminished 5th (same as augmented 4th)
perfect 5th (3 1/2 steps: 7 half steps)

6ths: minor 6th (4 steps: 8 half steps)
major 6th (4 1/2 steps: 9 half steps)

7ths: minor 7th (5 steps: 10 half steps)
major 7th (5 1/2 steps: 11 half steps)

Later on, however, you might want to work with compound intervals (an octave and larger).

- All that follows uses only natural notes: A B C D E F G (no sharps or flats).

  Play all diatonic 2nds up and down each of the five sets of two adjacent strings. Then play all the 3rds, 4ths, 5ths, and 6ths. Then play the 6ths again on two strings, skipping the one in between. Then play the 7ths on the same four sets of two non-adjacent strings (E & D; A & G; D & B; G & E).

  Could you improvise against any of the seven major modes with these double stops?

  Sure ya could!

  Try 3rds first because they're easy to play and sound good. Try 6ths on non-adjacent strings for the same reasons. Then maybe 4ths. Then 5ths. Then 6ths on adjacent strings. Then 7ths. And lastly, 2nds. You'll notice that all of this work involves parallel and similar motion.

B. The next step is to start moving from one kind of interval to another—3rd to a 6th, for example. This next step provides for contrary motion and oblique motion. (See examples that follow later).

- Here is a list of "interval moves":

2nd to 3rd;	2nd to 4th;	2nd to 5th;	2nd to 6th;	2nd to 7th
3rd to 2nd;	**3rd to 4th;**	3rd to 5th;	3rd to 6th;	3rd to 6th
4th to 2nd;	4th to 3rd;	**4th to 5th;**	4th to 6th;	4th to 7th
5th to 2nd;	5th to 3rd;	5th to 4th;	**5th to 6th;**	5th to 7th
6th to 2nd;	6th to 3rd;	6th to 4th;	6th to 5th;	**6th to 7th**
7th to 2nd;	7th to 3rd;	7th to 4th;	7th to 5th;	7th to 6th

  Question: Can you see why certain intervals are **bold**?

- Remember, all of this material can work for any and all of the seven modes of C major.

- Could you move from an interval to another kind and then to another kind? (three different intervals, i. e., 3rd, 6th, 4th). Sure ya could! (I wonder how long the list of "interval moves" would be using 3 intervals? Have you got a computer?) How about four or five or six or seven intervals? (Sorcerer's apprentice, watch out!) But enough is enough. Just remember: when you know all of your intervals, you'll know all of your intervals.

- Play and study the following examples:

Write the interval type and then play.

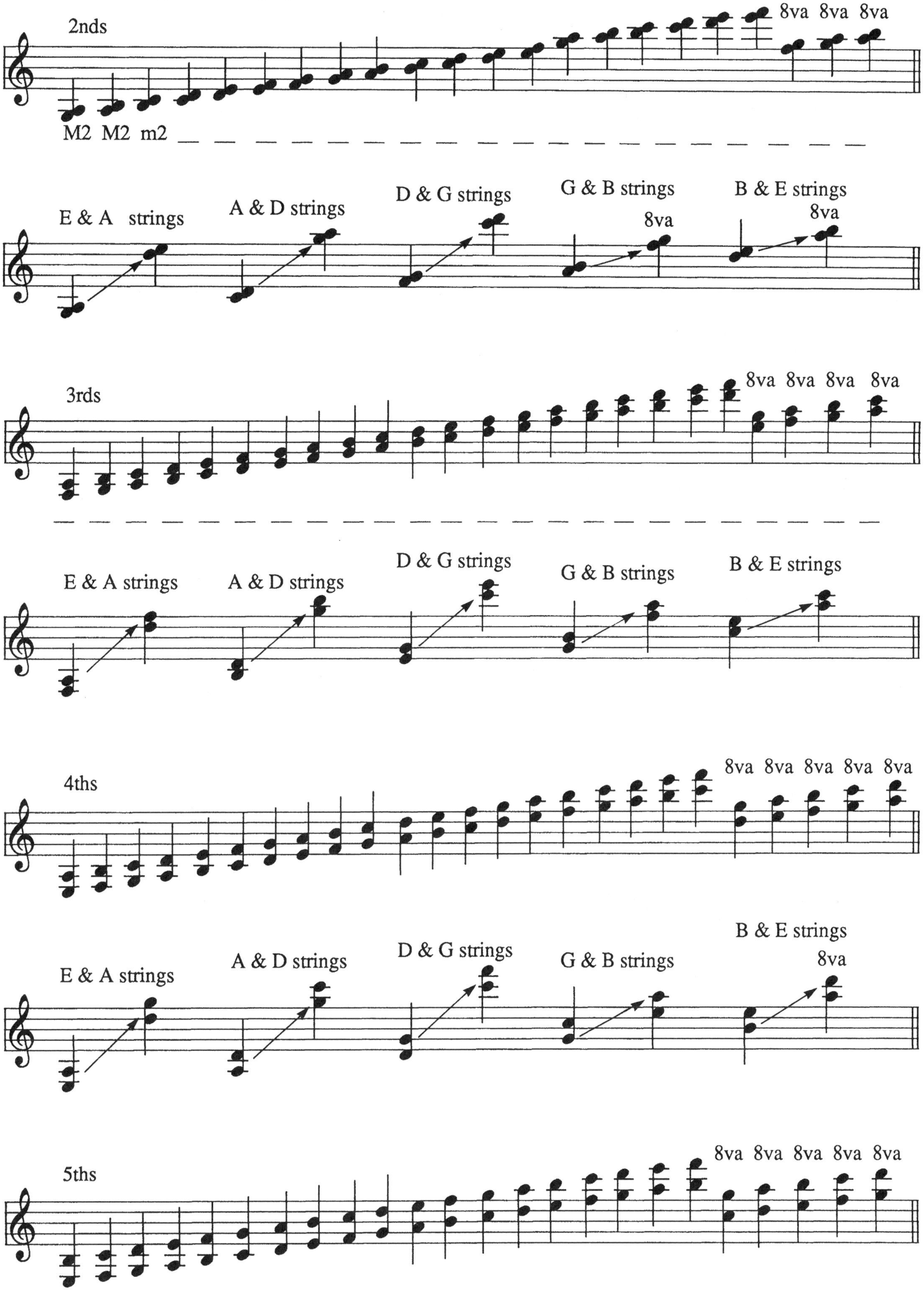
2nds
8va 8va 8va
M2 M2 m2
E & A strings
A & D strings
D & G strings
G & B strings
8va
B & E strings
8va
3rds
8va 8va 8va 8va
E & A strings
A & D strings
D & G strings
G & B strings
B & E strings
4ths
8va 8va 8va 8va 8va
E & A strings
A & D strings
D & G strings
G & B strings
B & E strings
8va
5ths
8va 8va 8va 8va 8va

E & A strings
A & D strings
D & G strings
G & B strings
B & E strings
8va
6ths
8va 8va 8va 8va 8va
Adjacent Strings
E & A strings
A & D strings
D & G strings
G & B strings
8va
B & E strings
8va
Non Adjacent strings
E & D strings
A & G strings
D & B strings
8va
G & E strings
8va
7ths
8va 8va 8va 8va 8va
Non Adjacent Strings
E & D strings
A & G strings
D & B strings
8va
G & E strings
8va

Optional: identify the interval type. Definitely *play*.

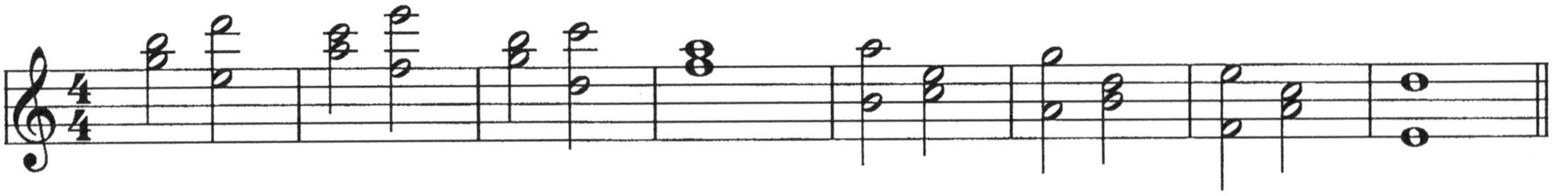

C. Now if someone played all of that material over an open pedal A string, we'd all know that he'd be playing in the A Aeolian mode. Right? We'd also see that he was playing three different parts, right? (Two melodies and a bass drone.) If this "someone" was interested, he might decide to explore this kind of playing a little bit every day for a long time, just to see what it could lead to. Now, maybe he might get tired of A Aeolian after a while. Maybe he'd decide to play in E Phrygian for a time (or retune the E string down to D for D Dorian.) Who knows what he might do? May be he'd even learn how to move the bass part around a bit. (then, there'd be three melodies! Not necessarily all moving at once.) Then one day, it might occur to him that he could try playing this way through a progression of chords using different scales and modes (not just the C major scale and its modes). Who knows?

Now, if someone did all of that, I wouldn't mind it at all. Would you mind it if someone did that? I thought so.

(A good horse runs at the shadow of the whip.)

The Open Position

The open position is the usual starting place in most guitar method books. (Hopefully, by this time you understand why this present volume doesn't start with open position!) By the open position, we mean the six open strings and frets 1, 2, 3, and 4. The open position amounts to a small melodic instrument unto itself, with a range of two octaves plus a major 3rd (E G#). Every note in the chromatic scale is present. Each note has only one location and one fingering with the exception of the B, which can either be played as an open string or on the 4th fret of the G string. Compared to the overall complexity of the entire guitar, the open position is a very simple (but none the less complete) melodic instrument.

In most method books the open position is used like training wheels on a bicycle: discarded as soon as possible. After you learn the C scale (and maybe a few other scales) you are usually encouraged to proceed to position playing, which is usually portrayed as much more important than the open position. You are also usually discouraged from using the open position as much as possible in favor of playing in one or another of the higher positions. Now to a certain extent, this approach makes sense and is fairly logical. However, I think in other ways it's not enough for someone who is *really* interested in learning as much about the guitar as possible. The open position is a fascinating area unto itself. It also happens to be a great preparation for the apparently awesome task of position playing. But this preparation aspect can only be appreciated if the open position is examined in great detail (which, as you may have gathered by now, is exactly what I'm proposing!) By great detail I mean:

1. Chromatic Scale
   * a. in octaves (great left hand exercise)
   * b. at other intervals (Perfect 4th up to a major 10th)
2. Two Whole-tone Scales
3. Three Symetrical Diminished Scales
4. Twelve Major Scales
5. Twelve Melodic Minor Scales
6. Twelve Harmonic Minor Scales
7. Twelve Pentatonic Scales (1, 2, 3, 5, 6)
8. Twelve Pentatonic Scales (1, 2 b3, 5, 6)
9. * All Triads and four-part Chord Arpeggios in all Keys

* Optional

At this point, I'm going to suggest that those of you who are just learning about modes, single-string and double-string soloing for the first time, skip this material for now. You can come back to it whenever you want. For now, just play the C major scale in open position and improvise on the vamps for each of the seven modes of C.

Then proceed to **Position Playing** and only work on the material in the section called "The Straight Path."

Observations

- The main difference between the open position and position playing (which follows, soon enough) is that in the open position, the open strings function for the notes that in position playing would require 1st and 4th finger stretches. (This may take a little time to understand.) From another angle: no finger stretches in open position.

- The open strings tend to ring out when we don't want them to. This means that we need to develop techniques of stopping open strings. This is usually accomplished with a left hand-finger. Finger-style people also have options with using right-hand fingers to stop open strings from vibrating. (See exercises that follow.)

- Interesting and very accessible possibilities of slurring (hammer-ons and pull-offs) exist in the open position.
  Check 'em out!

- In this approach to the open position there is one rule to be followed: same finger - same fret.

  A note on the 1st fret *must* be played with the 1st finger.
  A note on the 2nd fret *must* be played with the 2nd finger.
  A note on the 3rd fret *must* be played with the 3rd finger.
  A note on the 4th fret *must* be played with the 4th finger.

  NO EXCEPTIONS!

  Consequently, we will not explore counterpoint and harmony in the open position because the rule of same finger/same fret would make many voicings impossible. (Later on, of course, you could explore counterpoint and harmony in the open position. When you decide to do that, just use *any* fingers you have to for whatever the notes are.)

- In this particular approach, the open position is our first truly "chromatic area of substantial melodic possibilities." All scales, all modes, all arpeggios are there. (Think about what that means!)

- Since the only note that has two locations and two fingerings is the B (open string or 4th fret of G string), it would be a good idea to experiment with both possibilities when playing any scale, mode, or arpeggio that contains the note B (or Cb). Sometimes, one choice is obviously better than the other. Sometimes, both are about the same.

- A person could spend a whole lifetime playing only in the open position. (Imagine the joy of playing on a guitar with ten to eleven strings that had only four frets!)

- Sometimes people who write books make weird observations.

Ex. 1A

Ex. 1B

Ex. 2A

Ex. 2B

Ex. 3

Ex. 4A

Ex. 4B

Position Playing

On the guitar, a position means a section of the fingerboard covering six frets across all six strings. The range of a position is two octaves plus a P4 (29 half steps). In this range, every note in the chromatic scale is present. Twenty-four of the available pitches have only one location and one fingering. The other six pitches have two locations and two fingerings.

There are four possible left hand-finger alignments:

	1	2	3	4		(normal)	4 frets
1		2	3	4		(first finger stretch)	5 frets
	1	2	3		4	(fourth finger stretch)	5 frets
1		2	3		4	(double finger stretch)	6 frets

These four combine to give us:

1 1 2 3 4 4

The position you are in is determined by the fret just below the 2nd (middle) finger.

1 1 2 3 4 4
position (↑ under the second 1)

It's where the 1st finger normally falls. But since the 1st finger covers two frets, this is sometimes confusing. If you're playing the A Aeolian mode in fifth position, the low A is played with the 1st finger on the 5th fret of the low E string (normal placement of 1st finger for fifth position). But if you're playing an Ab Major scale in fifth position, the low Ab is played on the 4th fret of the low E string with the 1st finger (stretched placement of 1st finger in fifth position). Even though you're playing a note on the 4th fret, you're still in the fifth position. That is, of course, assuming that you play the Bb with your 2nd (middle) finger. If you play the Bb with your 3rd (ring) finger, then you're not in fifth position; you'd be in fourth.

From this we see that position is really determined by the placement of the 2nd and 3rd fingers (middle and ring fingers). Fifth position means:

1. 2nd finger on 6th fret
2. 3rd finger on 7th fret
3. 1st finger on 5th fret (normal); 1st finger on 4th fret (stretched)
4. 4th finger on 8th fret (normal); 4th finger on 9th fret (stretched)

Here are some **rules** that apply to position playing:

- Don't ever stretch between 2nd and 3rd finger
- Don't shift 2nd and 3rd finger up or down a fret (this amounts to changing positions)
- Don't use the same finger to play two consecutive scale degrees if there's another way to finger it. (Sometimes there is; sometimes there isn't.)

Here are some **suggestions** that apply to position playing:

1. Become as familiar as possible with all alternate fingerings in a position.

2. Be especially aware of alternate fingerings on the G and B strings. This is because of the fact that the 3rd interval between those strings (as opposed to the perfect 4th interval that occurs between all the other sets of adjacent strings) changes things around quite a bit.

3. Realize that a position contains the whole "chromatic universe" within the range (two octaves plus a perfect fourth). Consequently, this means that any position (and all positions) contains:

   - Chromatic Scale (12 notes)
   - Two Whole-tone Scales (6 notes each)
   - Three Symmetrical Diminished Scales (8 note scales)
   - Twelve Major Scales (7-note scales)
   - Twelve Melodic Minor Scales (7-note scales)
   - Twelve Harmonic Minor Scales (7-note scales)
   - Twelve Pentatonic Scales (5-note scales)
   - All triads and four part chord arpeggios in all keys
   - Plus a whole lot more...

   I'm sure by now you can see the vastness of this project called position playing.

4. In approaching all of this material, it would be good to keep in mind that (as often happens) there are two different approaches, both of which are important. For example, let's take the major scale. The first approach would be to keep the major scale the same, and change the position (i.e., C Major Scale in each of the twelve positions). The second approach would be to keep the position the same and change the scale (i.e., all twelve major scales in one position). This principle of "keep one thing the same while the other changes; then change the one thing while the other stays the same" is a very important concept when working with the guitar. You'll see it popping up time and again.

5. Since most guitarists don't have large hands, it might make sense to start extensive work in one position higher up on the fingerboard (seventh position or higher). The reason for this is that the higher the position,the closer together are the frets. Thus, a higher position would be physically a bit easier, particularly considering the 1st and 4th finger stretches. With this approach, you would start with a relatively high position and gradually work your way down to the lower positions as the left hand got accustomed to the 1st and 4th finger stretches.

6. Position playing involves a lot of what is often called "Finger-pattern memory". It's a very big and important part of guitar playing. However, don't forget the *names* of the notes. And don't forget the *degree* of the note relative to the root of the scale or arpeggio. (The same applies to chords.) If your aim is to be thorough, remember that no one thing or approach is the most important or the best. All things and/or approaches are important.

7. Position playing is an extremely disciplined study. It's a great thing to work with when you feel in the mood to be disciplined. On the other hand, when you're "playing", you certainly don't want to confine yourself unnecessarily. Position playing is sort of like a"gear" that you need to be able to "shift" into or out of at will (for as long or short a time as is necessary).

8. There is no direct relationship between how well you know position playing and how well you can improvise. On the other hand, it should be easy to see that there could quite easily be at least an indirect relationship! Or, to put it another way: if you improvise, knowing position playing very well sure helps.

Things to Do

- Go through the material listed under no. 3 of **suggestions.**
- Play through any (or all) Jazz standard(s) keeping entirely in one position while you're improvising. (Remember: anything you want is there, somewhere!)
- Play through things like Rhythm Changes and Blues Changes all in one position. If you wanted, you could stay in the same position and transpose either or both forms (Blues, Rhythm Changes) to all twelve keys. Or change the position and keep the key the same.
- When working with scales (and especially modes), as soon as you "know the fingerings," start *improvising.* Explore interval leaps - patterns, anything you can think of and/or hear. If you just practice playing up and down the scale or mode, your improvising will sound that way. (This is one of the biggest problems that beginning and intermediate guitarists have with improvising. They just play scales up and down and play arpeggios up and down. That's barely enough to get you "in the near vicinity of the ballpark"! It certainly isn't enough to "get you into the ballpark" and it's light years away from "actually playing the ballgame"!)

The Straight Path

Learn fingerings for the C major scale in positions one through twelve. Improvise against seven major mode vamps in all twelve positions. (seven modes times twelve positions equals 84 possibilities.)

Optional: Learn fingerings for all twelve major scales in the position of your choice. (seventh position or higher, unless your fingers are as long as bananas!) Improvise on all 84 modes (seven modes times twelve key equals 84 possibilities.)

Idea: Make tapes of pedal roots at different tempos. Get three 60-minute cassette tapes. Record two 15-minute roots on each side. That would be four roots per cassette. Three cassettes would be enough for all twelve roots.

Combination Playing: "The Realm of the Electric Ice-skating Rink"

Combination playing is what guitarists do the most when they play. They don't just play on one string; they don't just play in a position. They mix it all up; they move around. Hopefully, they follow the music, which takes them wherever it needs to be taken. (Hopefully!)

I think it should be fairly clear by now that a lot of playing up and down the individual strings *combined* with a lot of playing in positions would add up to the largest possible preparation for combination playing. What we are looking for as improvisers is the greatest possible feeling of freedom with respect to whatever area of the fingerboard the music happens to take us. (Thus, "The Realm of the Electric Ice-skating Rink)."

The principles of combination playing are fairly simple. Let's take our old friend, the C major scale, out for a walk:

1. Play the C scale only using two notes per string:

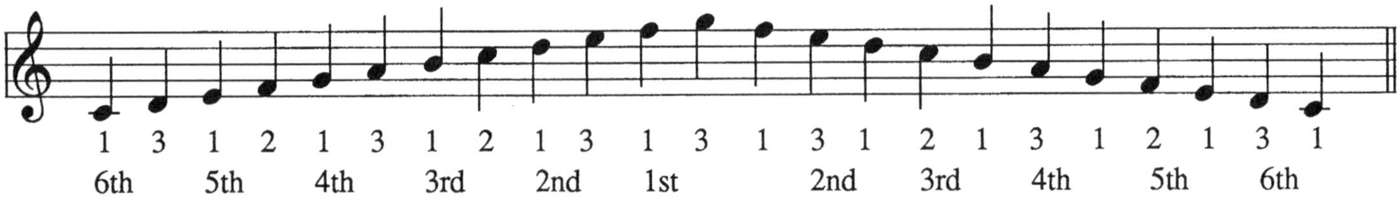
1 3 1 2 1 3 1 2 1 3 1 3 1 3 1 2 1 3 1 2 1 3 1
6th 5th 4th 3rd 2nd 1st 2nd 3rd 4th 5th 6th

Notice that with this fingering, you move *down* the neck as the scale goes *up;* and that you move *up* the neck as the scale goes *down*! Isn't that interesting? I wonder what might be the use of such a movement. What do you think?

2. Play the C scale starting on *any* note (low E string) and play three notes on every string. You'll notice that these fingerings look just like position playing until you get to the B string. Then, you have to shift to a higher position for the last two strings. This kind of fingering would come in handy if you wanted to play the following:

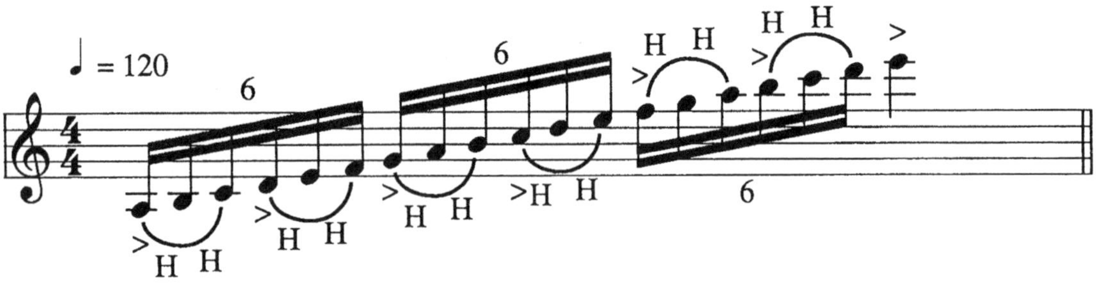
♩ = 120
6
6
6
H H
H H
H H
H H
H H
H H

So, from this example we can see that rhythmical groupings are an important consideration. Three notes per string makes sense for triplets, sextuplets, etc. Also, we see that articulation can be important. In the above example, notes 1, 4, 7, 10, 13, 16, and 19 are attacked; all others are to be slurred (hammer-ons).

3. Suppose you want to play 16th notes; try these examples:

Ex. A

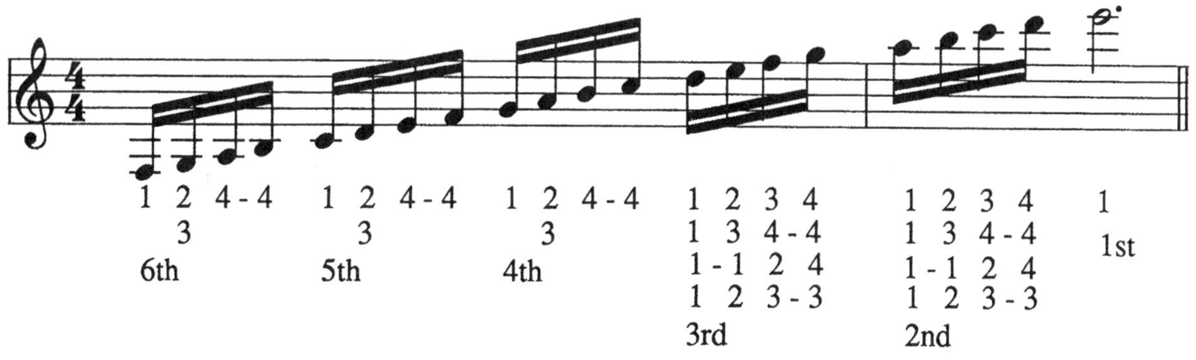

1 2 4-4 1 2 4-4 1 2 4-4 1 2 3 4 1 2 3 4 1
3 3 3 1 3 4-4 1 3 4-4 1st
6th 5th 4th 1-1 2 4 1-1 2 4
1 2 3-3 1 2 3-3
3rd 2nd

Ex. B

2nd Pos.
4th Pos.
6th Pos.
7th Pos.
9th Pos.
1 2 4 1 - 1 2 4 1 - 1 2 4 1 - 1 2 4 2 - 2 4 1 2 4

Ex. C

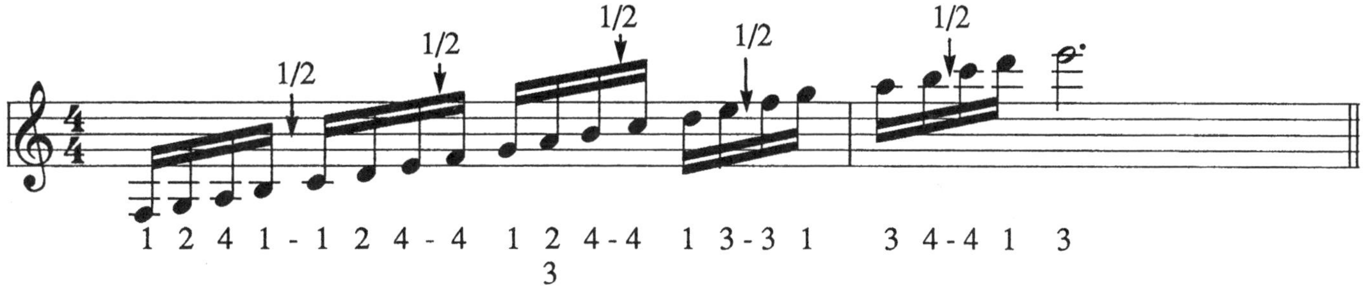

1/2
1/2
1/2
1/2
1/2
1 2 4 1 - 1 2 4 - 4 1 2 4-4 1 3-3 1 3 4-4 1 3
3

In example A, the idea is four notes per *string*.
In example B, the idea is four notes per *position*.
In example C. the idea is to *shift positions* between half steps.,

4. Now, experiment with playing the same passage many different ways by combining the ideas of examples A, B, and C.

So, to review:

1. Notes per string: two, three, four, (five, six)
2. Notes per position: two, three, four, five, six
3. Shift positions by half steps (or *any* interval, for that matter!)
4. Rhythmical considerations: triplets, 16ths, etc.

Playing scales up and down with these ideas is interesting, but unfortunately, when you're improvising, it doesn't "come up much in conversation." So, start leaping around to search out melodies and interesting patterns. (And put on your finger-skates, because you're just about to enter the"Realm O' the Rink)."

To Do:

- Experiment with all possible scales, modes and arpeggios using the entire fingerboard.
- Improvise on Vamps, Standard Tunes, Blues, and Rhythm Changes using the entire fingerboard.

The Straight Path

Improvise on modes of C major scale using the entire fingerboard.

The Approach: Take 2, Take 3

We've taken the C major scale and its modes all the way through "The Approach." Now, go back to the beginning and go through the same procedures using the **C melodic minor** scale and its modes. (You'll probably want to use "the Straight Path" sections.) When you've completed that, start back at the beginning again, but this (third) time, use the **C harmonic minor** scale and its modes. (Work *especially* on the modes built on I, IV, V, VI.)

- It's absolutely amazing what happens when you change one note in a major scale. (E changes to Eb for melodic minor.)
- It's also absolutely amazing what happens when you change one note in a melodic minor scale. (A changes to Ab for harmonic minor.)
- You might also work with other seven- note scales. For example, C D E F G Ab B C *or* C Db E F G Ab B C.
- Sheets on C melodic minor and C harmonic minor follow:

Melodic Minor Modes

Melodic Minor (Jazz Minor)

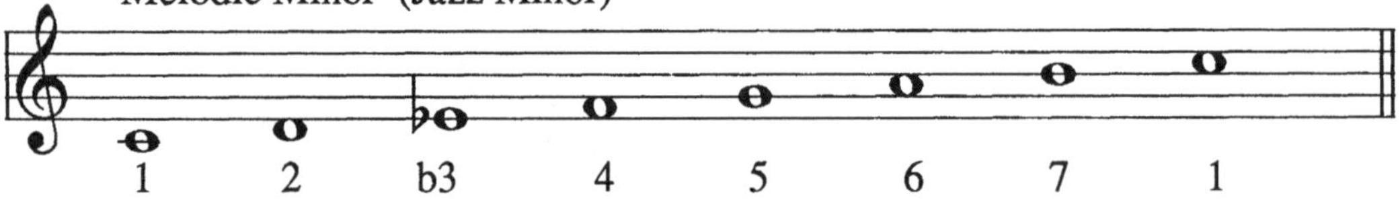
1 2 b3 4 5 6 7 1

Dorian b2 (Phyrgian ♮ 6)

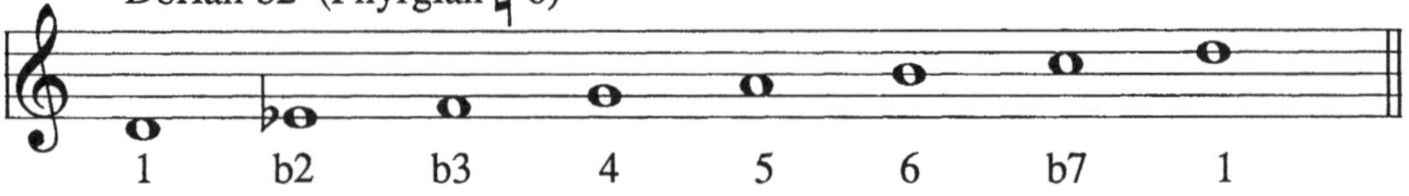
1 b2 b3 4 5 6 b7 1

Lydian Augmented

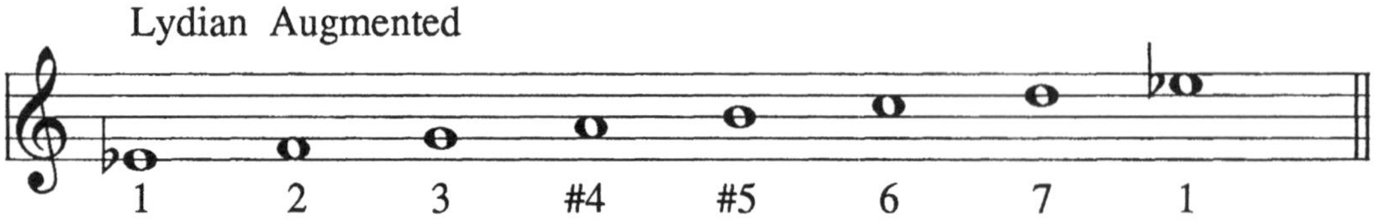
1 2 3 #4 #5 6 7 1

Lydian b7 (Overtone Scale)

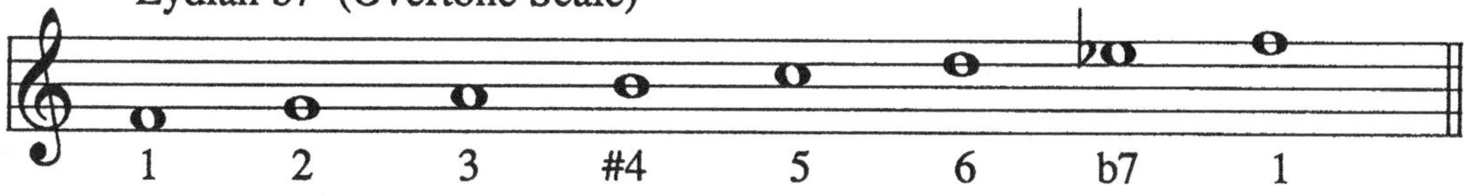
1 2 3 #4 5 6 b7 1

Aeolian Major (Mixolydian b6)

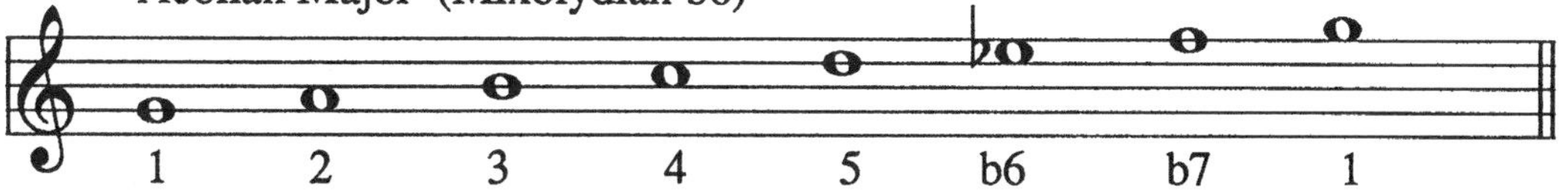
1 2 3 4 5 b6 b7 1

Locrian ♮ 2

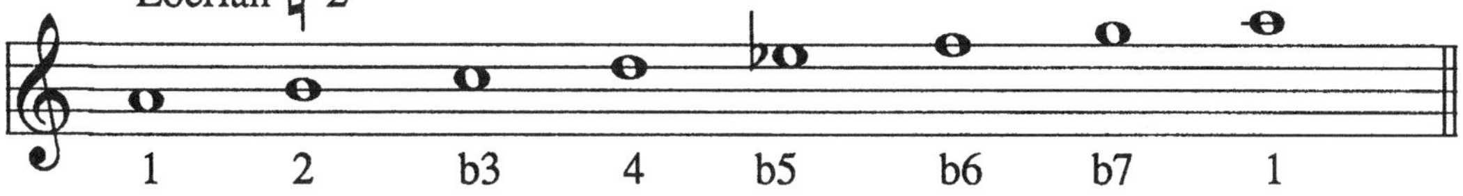
1 2 b3 4 b5 b6 b7 1

Altered Dominant (Super Locrian)

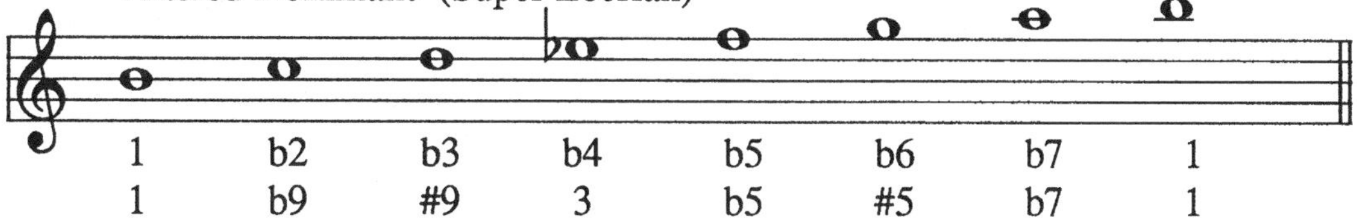
1 b2 b3 b4 b5 b6 b7 1
1 b9 #9 3 b5 #5 b7 1

Melodic Minor Vamps

Melodic Minor

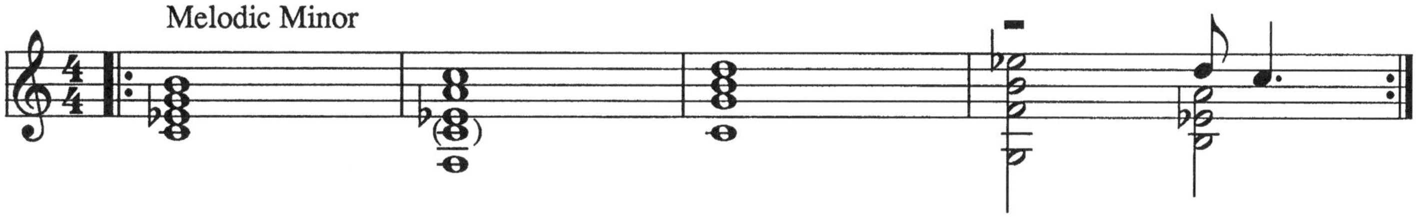

6th=D Phrygian ♮ 6

6th=Eb Lydian Augmented

1.
2.

Lydian b7
Ex. 1
Ex. 2
Aeolian Major
Altered Dominant
B7 Alt.
E-

Harmonic Minor Modes

★ = useful modes (★) = slightly less important but still useful

Harmonic Minor

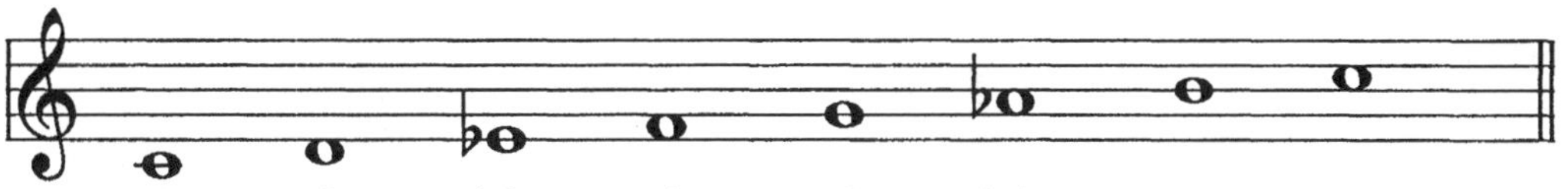

1 2 b3 4 5 b6 7 1 ★

Locrian ♮6

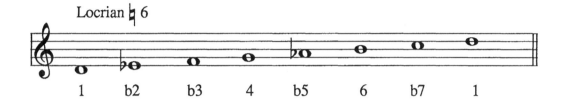

1 b2 b3 4 b5 6 b7 1

Ionian Augmented

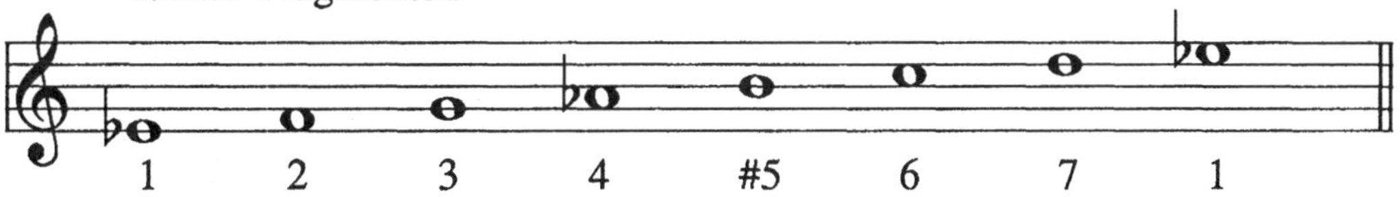

1 2 3 4 #5 6 7 1

Dorian #4 (Overtone Minor)

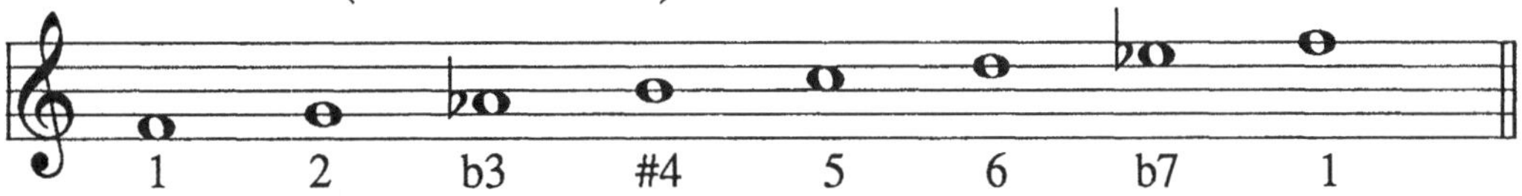

1 2 b3 #4 5 6 b7 1 (★)

Phrygian Major

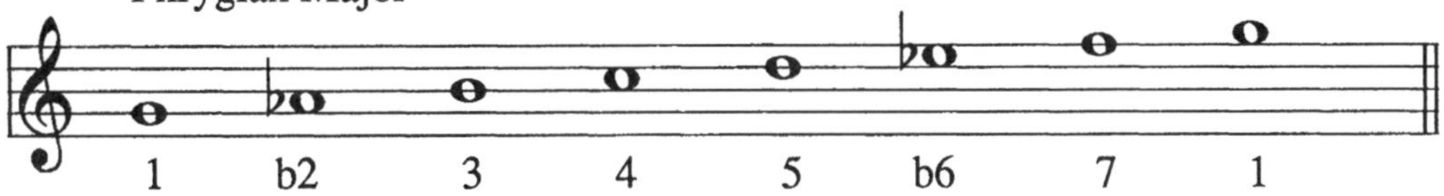

1 b2 3 4 5 b6 7 1 ★

Lydian #9

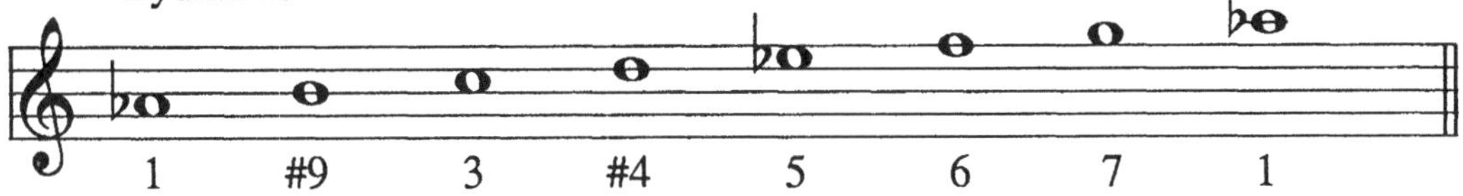

1 #9 3 #4 5 6 7 1 (★)

Altered Dominant bb7

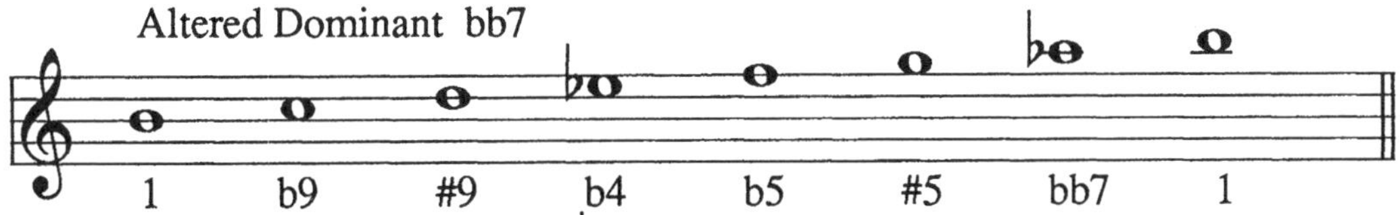

1 b9 #9 b4 b5 #5 bb7 1

♮3 #11 b13

Harmonic Minor Vamps

Harmonic Minor
Ex. 1
Ex. 2

6th=D
Locrian♮ 6

Ionian Augmented

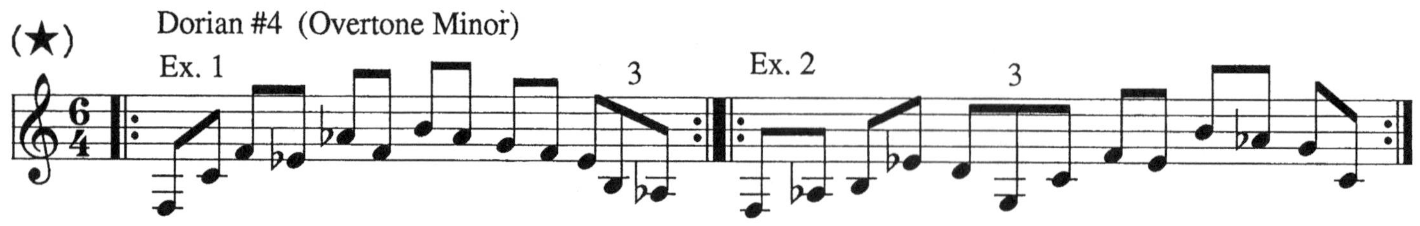
Dorian #4 (Overtone Minor)
Ex. 1
3
Ex. 2
3

Phrygian Major

Lydian #9

Altered Dominant bb7

What Next?

At this point, I think it makes sense to mention something. Our approach has been primarily derivative so far. (The modes were *derived* from C major scale, C melodic minor, C harmonic minor, etc.) It would be a good idea to go through the same material again, but this time, approaching it in a parallel fashion. That means: all the modes from the same root. You might choose to pick C as the root since you probably know that key fairly well by now. Personally, I think it might be even better to pick either E or A. These notes are the two lowest open strings. The idea here is that it would be very convenient to have a low, open-string root in going through the parallel approach. This is particularly true of harmonic material, since you'll have either four or five of the higher strings to play the voicings, as well as the low, open-string root to sound against any voicing you want. That might come in very handy.

E Ionian	E Dorian b2	E Phrygian major
E Dorian	E Lydian augmented	E Lydian #2
E Phrygian	E Lydian b7	E whole tone
E Lydian	E Aeolian major	E pentatonic (chinese) 1 2 3 5 6
E Mixoloydian	E Locrian ♮2	E pentatonic (japanese) 1 2 b3 5 6
E Aeolian	E altered dominant bb7	E sym. diminished whole step, half step
E Locrian	E harmonic minor	E sym. diminished (dom.) half step, whole step
E melodic minor	E Dorian #4	

Examples:

1. Play the melody to "Happy Birthday" in E Ionian. Transpose it to the other 17 7-note modes.

2. Write a simple melody in E Ionian that uses all the notes (seven) at least twice each. Transpose to the 17 other seven-note modes.

3. Go back to playing up and down a single string, using all the material, then play the other five strings. Then five sets of two adjacent strings. Then all the above material in open position. Then in one position. Then take a break!

4. Explore counterpoint and harmonic material from all above modes and scales for at least 20 years.

Next "What Next?"

The question remains: "What about all the other keys?" (And what a great question it is!) I'm not one for schedules, particularly, but a few interesting numerical coincidences might be worth mentioning at this point:

Time	**Musical Material**
7 days in a week	7 modes of major, melodic and harmonic minor
4 weeks in a month	4 triads; 4 families of 7th chords
4 seasons in a year	
12 months in a year etc., etc., etc...	12 keys; 12 positions on the guitar etc., etc., etc....

You get the idea.
I think much can be deduced
from what has been supplied
and/or inferred
from what has been implied.

Analyze and identify all of the following open-string intervals:

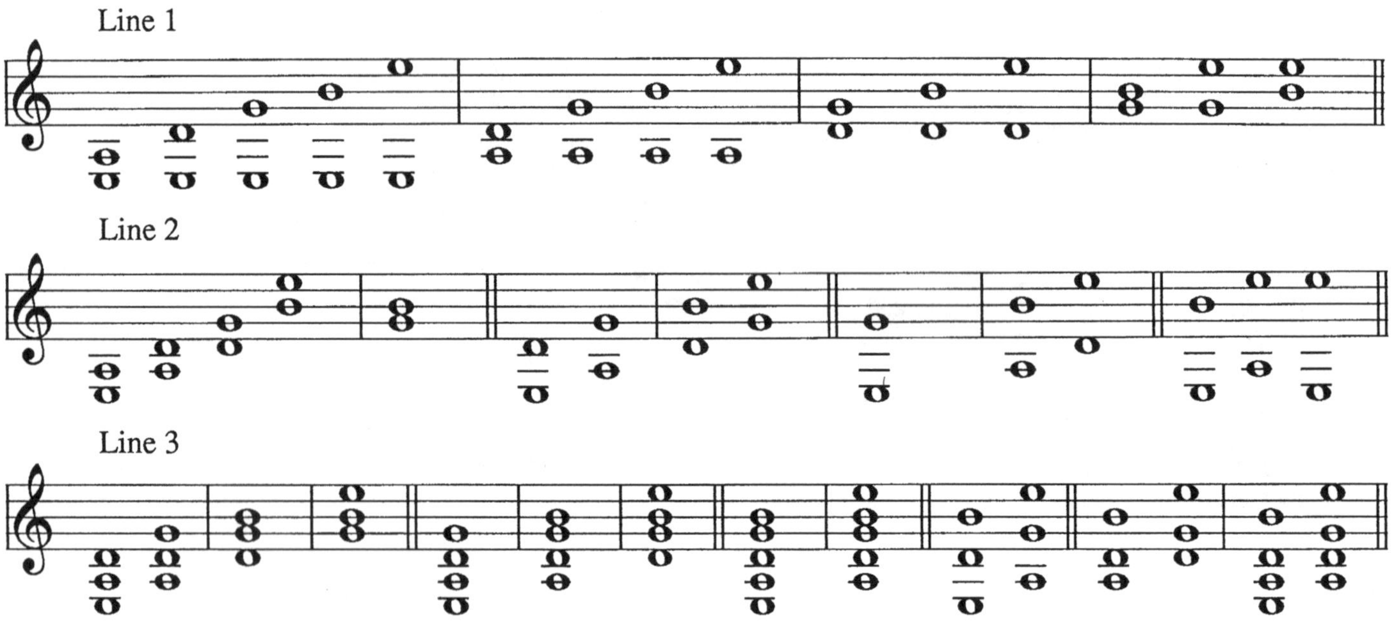
Line 1
Line 2
Line 3

1. Do you understand why the bar lines are placed where they are?
2. How about the double bar lines?
3. Can you explain the relationship of line 2 to line 1?
4. Other interval combinations have been omitted. Why?
5. To what extent does your harmonic (and contrapuntal) skill depend on knowing these intervals?
6. What would happen to these intervals if the guitar were tuned E A D G C F (all perfect 4ths)?
7. Have you suddenly decided to become a short-order cook?

II. MATERIALS

Triads

There are four types of triads: major, minor, augmented, and diminished. These four are the result of combining major and minor 3rd intervals.

Major Triad	**Minor Triad**	**Augmented Triad**	**Diminished Triad**
M3 + m3	m3 + M3	M3 + M3	m3 + m3
C-E E-G	C-Eb Eb-G	C-E E-G#	C-Eb Eb-Gb

Triads have three inversions:

Root Position				**1st Inversion**				**2nd Inversion**			
G	G	G#	Gb	C	C	C	C	E	Eb	E	Eb
E	Eb	E	Eb	G	G	G#	Gb	C	C	C	C
C	C	C	C	E	Eb	E	Eb	G	G	G#	Gb

Triads can also be spread in different ways:

3	5	1	5	1	3	3	5	1
5	1	3	3	5	1	5	1	3
1	3	5	OCTAVE			OCTAVE		
			1	3	5	1	3	5

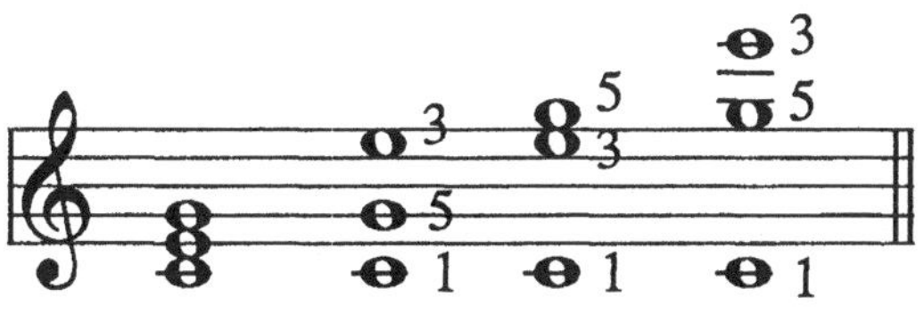

3
5
1
5
3
1
3
5
1

All inversions can be spread these ways.

Triads can also have a note doubled when you need four parts:

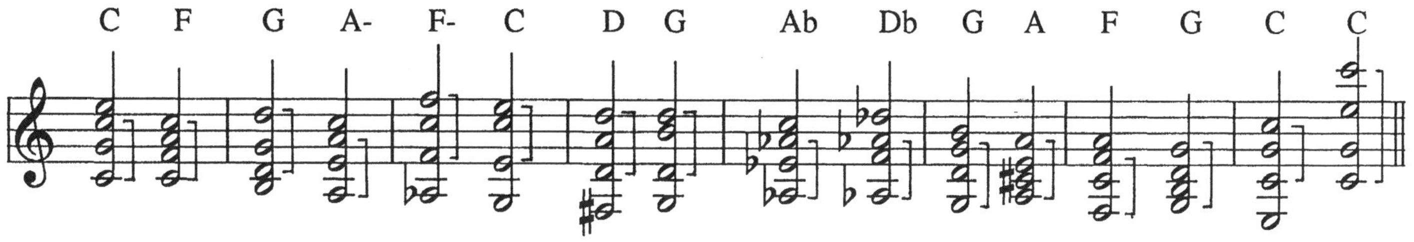

C F G A- F- C D G Ab Db G A F G C C

Now, go ahead and learn all C major, C minor, C augmented, and C diminished triads, all inversions, all registers, all locations, in closed as well as spread voicings that follow:

Optional: Figure out numbers of locations for minor, augmented, and diminished as was done in major triads.

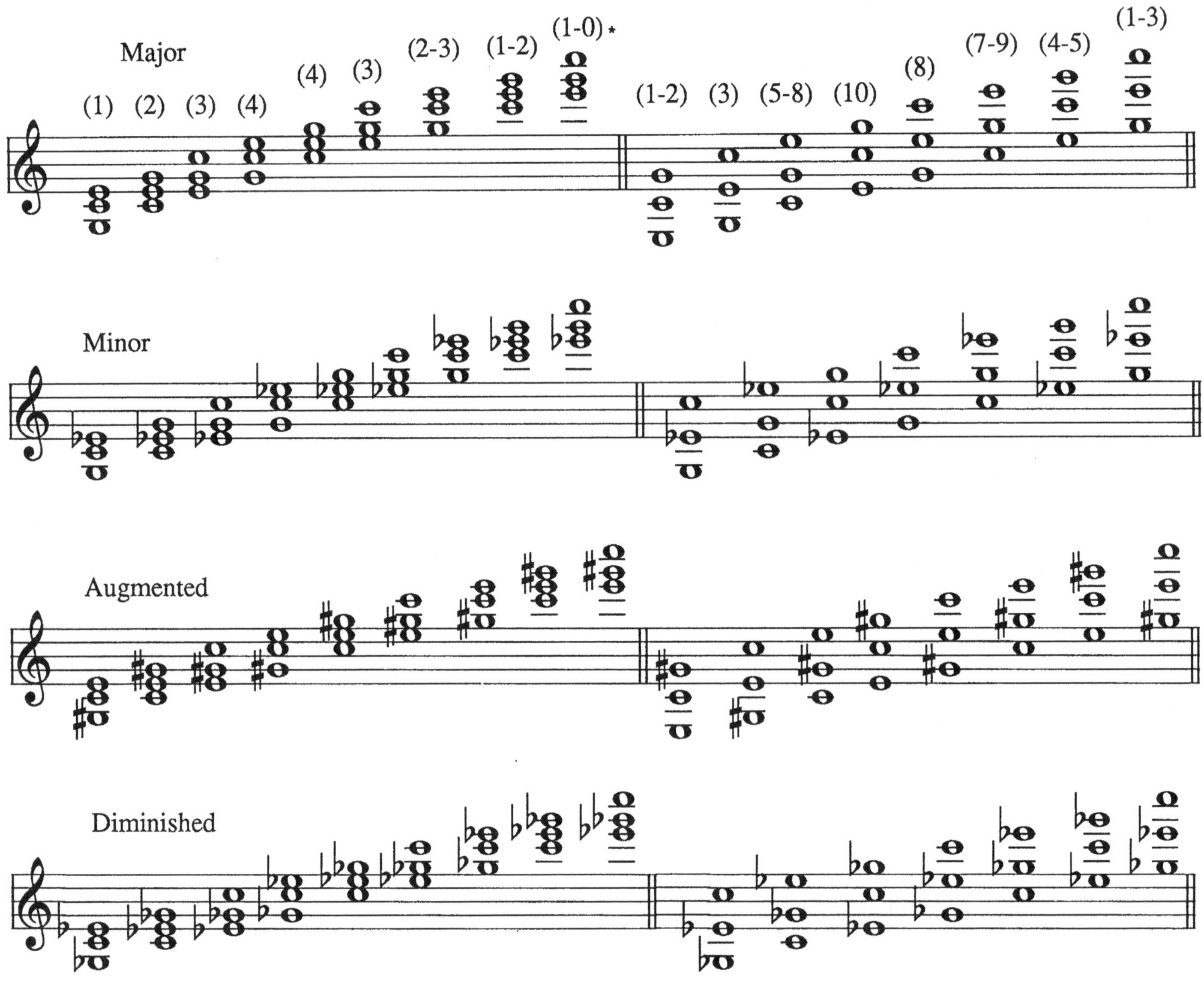
Major
(1) (2) (3) (4) (4) (3) (2-3) (1-2) (1-0)*
(1-2) (3) (5-8) (10) (8) (7-9) (4-5) (1-3)
Minor
Augmented
Diminished

It's probably easier to do the closed voicings (left side) for all four triads before doing the spread voicings (right side).

* These numbers indicate the number of possible fingerings for each voicing (which may vary depending on the number of frets on any given guitar).

Four triads from twelve roots makes 48 triads altogether.

C	C-	C+	C°	Eb	Eb-	Eb+	Eb°
F	F-	F+	F°	Ab	Ab-	Ab+	Ab°
Bb	Bb-	Bb+	Bb°	Db	Db-	Db+	Db°
F#	F#-	F#+	F#°	A	A-	A+	A°
B	B-	B+	B°	D	D-	D+	D°
E	E-	E+	E°	G	G-	G+	G°

These 48 triads can be randomly arranged to make vast numbers of "triad rows." (Use all 48 triads, but only once each.)

Bb+ Db E- F° D B+ Eb° F#- Bb- F+ E Ab° F#+ A G- Db°

C° Ab+ F# A- B° D+ F- E° C Ab+ G° A+ B- Eb C+ D°

F Db- E+ A° D- Eb+ Bb° G Bb G+ F#° Eb- Ab Db+ C- B

(Each row can be *re-arranged* in a vast number of ways.)

We can try to voice-lead the whole progression. Move each triad to the next with the least amount of movement. To do this, we:

1. Look for common tone(s), which is a note that is contained in two different triads. (Vertical lines are omitted for clarity. Read all triads vertically.)

	G	G	G#	Gb	Ab	A	Ab	A	A	Ab	G#	A
	E	Eb	E	Eb	Eb	E	E	Eb	F	F	E	F#
common tone C	C -	C -	C -	C -	C -	C -	C -	C -	C -	C -	C -	C
	ROOTS				3RDS				5THS			

The common tone must remain in the same voice: bass, middle, or top. The other two voices then move to the other two notes in the chord:

G	Ab	G -	G	F#
E	Eb -	Eb	D	D#
C -	C	Bb	B -	B

Sometimes, there could be two common tones:

G -	G -	G -	G
E -	E	Eb -	Eb
C	B -	B	C

2. Look for a half step, if you don't find a common tone:

G -	F#	G	F	G -	Gb
E	D	E	D	E -	Eb
C	A	C -	B	C	Bb

sometimes you might have two half steps, or even all three:

G -	Ab
E -	Eb
C -	C

Proper voice leading involves the least amount of combined melodic movement in all three voices:

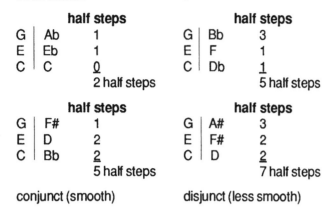

		half steps				half steps
G	Ab	1		G	Bb	3
E	Eb	1		E	F	1
C	C	0		C	Db	1
		2 half steps				5 half steps

		half steps				half steps
G	F#	1		G	A#	3
E	D	2		E	F#	2
C	Bb	2		C	D	2
		5 half steps				7 half steps

conjunct (smooth)   disjunct (less smooth)

Things to Do:

1. Now, go back to the "triad row" and voice-lead through the entire progression. (48 triads)
2. Now, play it backwards.
3. Start with a different inversion of the very first chord and go through the sequence again.
4. Play it backwards.
5. Start the sequence with a spread triad voicing and go through the whole sequence again.
6. Guess what now?
7. Can you see other things to do?

If you feel that you need to write them out on paper, go right ahead. That's a great thing to do. (This way, if you lose your place or something else weird happens, you've got it down on paper.) But as soon as you can, it's really good to go through these sequences just from the chord symbols.

Also, it's a good idea to have a notebook and/or music paper at hand when you are working with triads this way. You may come across some voicings for part of the progression that you really like. When this happens, write them down immediately. Don't just write the chord symbols. Take the time to write the exact voicings, because inversions can really change the sound of a progression. You can use these little "gems" for songs and/or pieces later on.

Observations

1. Augmented triads are tricky because the inversions on a given set of strings are all the same.
2. Diminished triads are tricky because the inversions on a given set of strings are all different.
3. It's easier to hear voices move with spread triads than with closed triads because there's more room between each voice.
4. This approach to triads is somewhat "dry" and a bit too theoretical for some people. Other people find it interesting because they understand that they are dealing with all of a large (but finite) number of possible units with almost infinite possible combinations.
5. There is a lot more to triadic harmony than many people would suspect.
6. Since most 7th chords consist of a triad plus one other note, this means that if you know your triads well, you already know about 75% of the 7th chords.

7. We usually think of harmony as beginning with triads. Intervals are really the beginning of harmony, but triad terminology conveys more information with shorter symbols.

8. When we get to the harmonic material derived from major, melodic minor, and harmonic minor scales, I suspect that you'll be glad you've worked with this approach to triads first. It also wouldn't surprise me if, after working with the harmonic material derived from the scales, you might decide to do some more work with the present approach to triads. It wouldn't surprise me at all.

More to Do with Triads

1. Root Progressions

Cycle 2: C Db D Eb E F Gb G Ab A Bb B
Cycle 7: C B Bb A Ab G Gb F E Eb D Db

```
                                                      (D#)
*(alternate) Cycle 3: C E G B D F# A C# E G# B Eb Gb Bb Db F Ab C Eb G Bb D F A
```

```
                                                          (Fb)
(alternate) Cycle 6: C A F D Bb G Eb C Ab F Db Bb Gb Eb Cb Ab E C# A F# D B G E
```

Cycle 4: C F Bb Eb Ab Db Gb B E A D G
Cycle 5: C G D A E B F# C# G# D# A# E#

```
                          (A#)      (G#)          (E#)     (D#)       (C#)
(alternate) Cycle 4: C F B E Bb Eb A D Ab Db G C F# B F Bb E A Eb Ab D G Db Gb
```

```
                          (Abb)     (Bbb)     (Cb)          (Ebb)      (Fb)
(alternate) Cycle 5: C Gb Db G D Ab Eb A E Bb F B F# C G Db Ab D A Eb Bb E B F
```

2. Tonic Systems

2 Tonic	C	F#				
3 Tonic	C	E	G#			
4 Tonic	C	Eb	Gb	A		
6 Tonic	C	D	E	F#	G#	A#

Also, all of the above retrograde.

All these progressions can be done with any of the four types of triads.
All these progressions can be done with any mixture of two types.
All these progressions can be done with any mixture of three types.
All these progressions can be done with any mixture of all four types.

3. Cadences

1 4 5 1 in Major	C F G C
1 4 5 1 in Melodic Minor	C- F G C-
1 4 5 1 in Harmonic Minor	C- F- G C-
1 4 5 1 in Natural Minor	C- F- G- C-

Optional: Could 1 4 5 1 cadences occur in other modes?
Could other cadences occur in other modes?

BONUS: I almost forgot to mention it: triads can be be arpeggiated!
(Maybe you had almost forgotten, too?)

* Alternate cycles contain two alternating intervals. For example, (alternate) cycle 3 alternates between major and minor 3rd.

7th Chords

What follows are some pages of important 7th chords in three different voicings: Drop 2, Drop 3, and Drop 2 and 4. (If you're interested, you might try Drop 2 and 3. Some of them are useful.)

4-way close **Drop 2** **Drop 3** **Drop 2 and 4** **Drop 2 and 3**

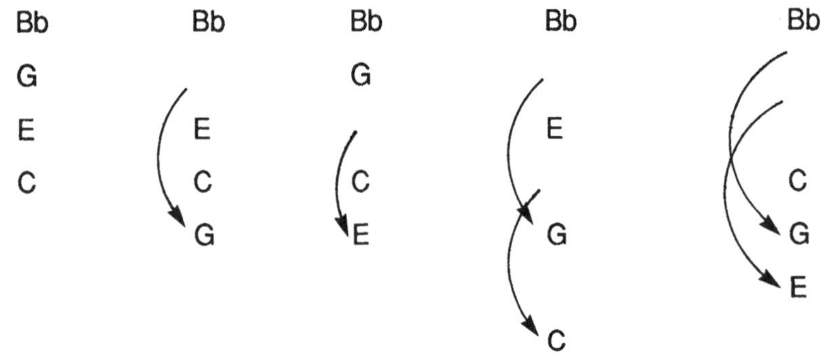

Bb G E C
Bb E C G
Bb G C E
Bb E G C
Bb C G E

All four inversions are shown for each chord. (The remaining voicings that are lower and higher need to be learned as well: don't forget, this is a do-it-yourself book!)

Question: How much of the material in the triad sections of this book would it be possible to apply to 7th chords?

DROP 2

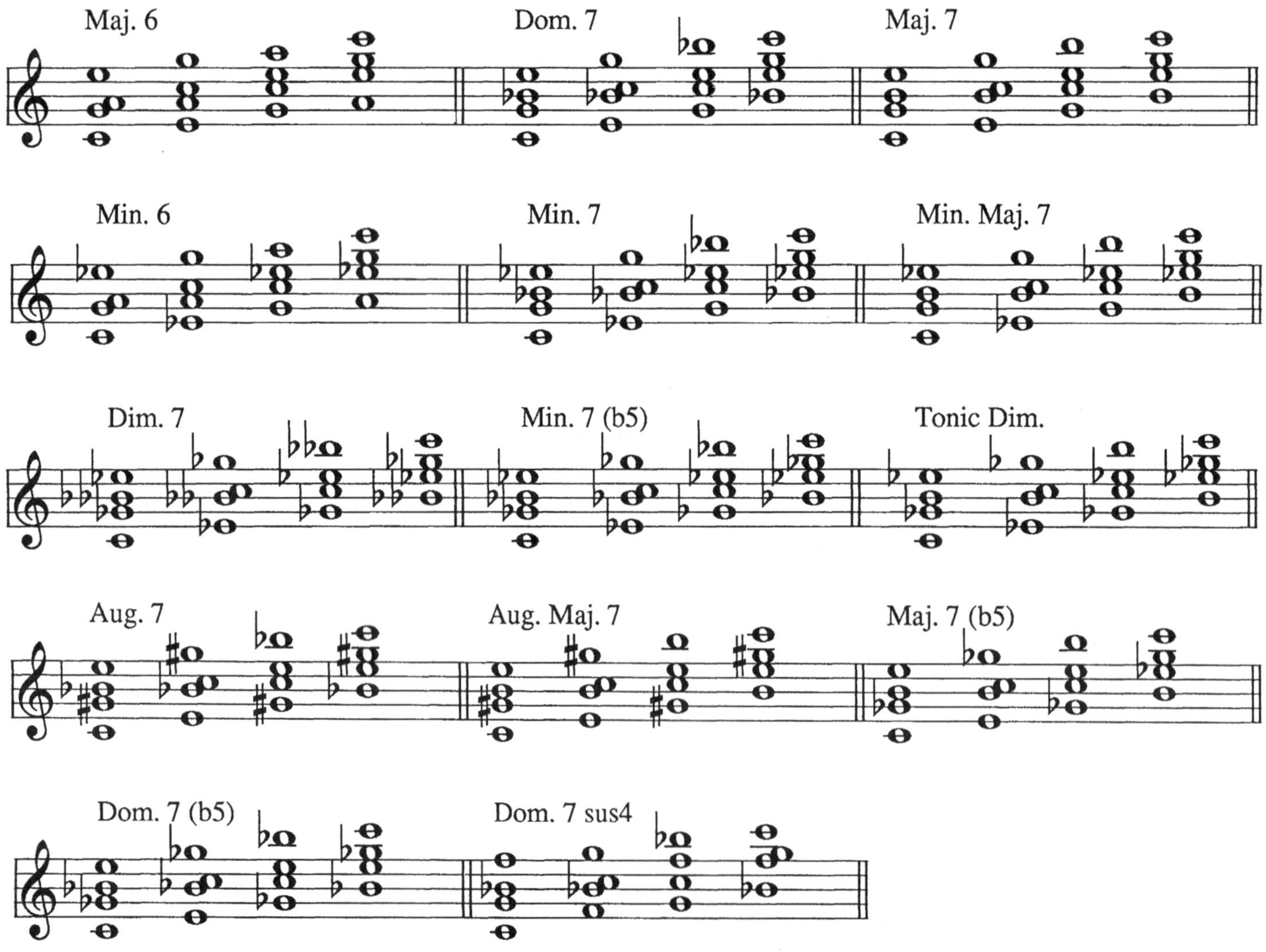

Maj. 6
Dom. 7
Maj. 7
Min. 6
Min. 7
Min. Maj. 7
Dim. 7
Min. 7 (b5)
Tonic Dim.
Aug. 7
Aug. Maj. 7
Maj. 7 (b5)
Dom. 7 (b5)
Dom. 7 sus4

DROP 3

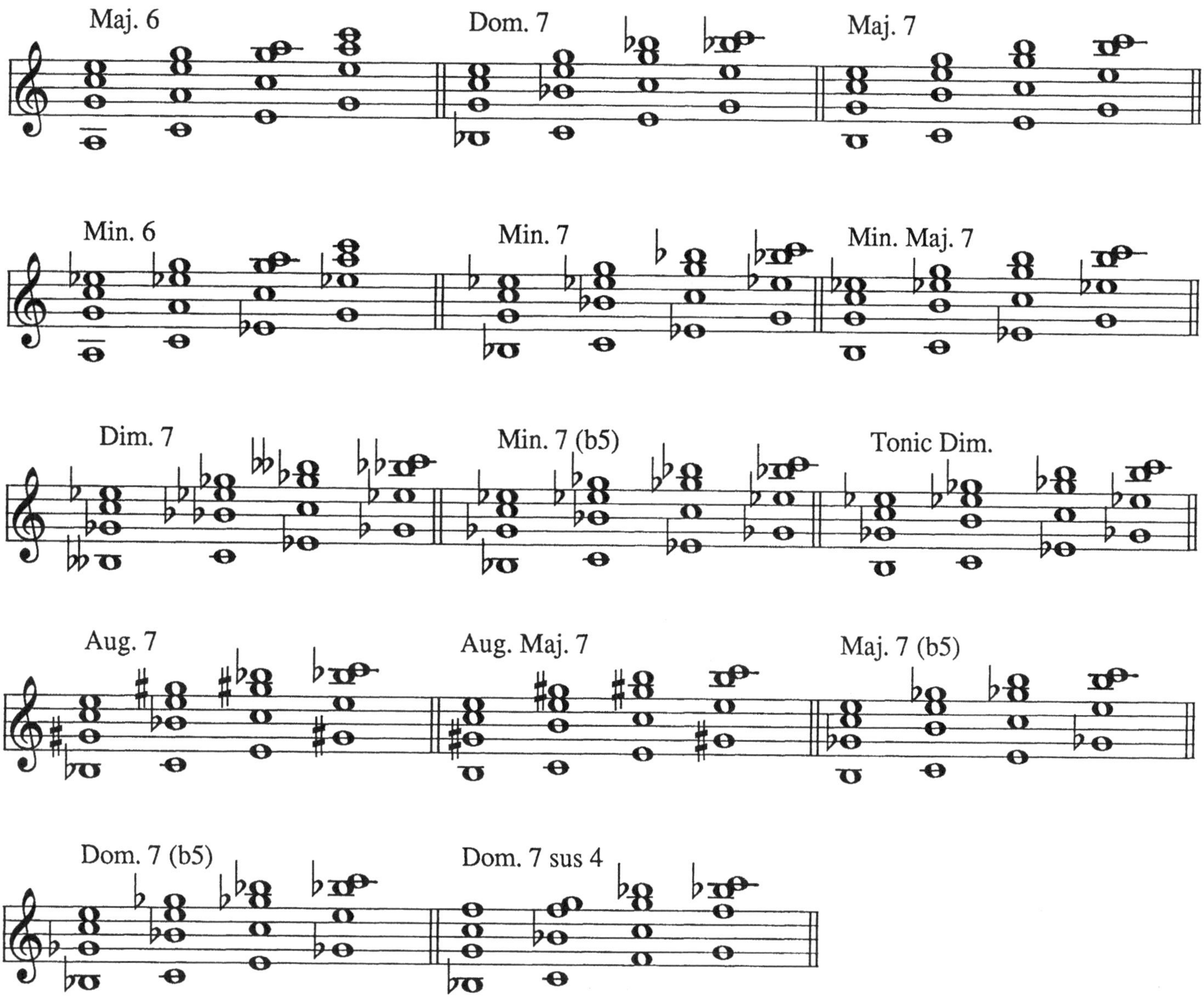
Maj. 6
Dom. 7
Maj. 7
Min. 6
Min. 7
Min. Maj. 7
Dim. 7
Min. 7 (b5)
Tonic Dim.
Aug. 7
Aug. Maj. 7
Maj. 7 (b5)
Dom. 7 (b5)
Dom. 7 sus 4

DROP 2 and 4

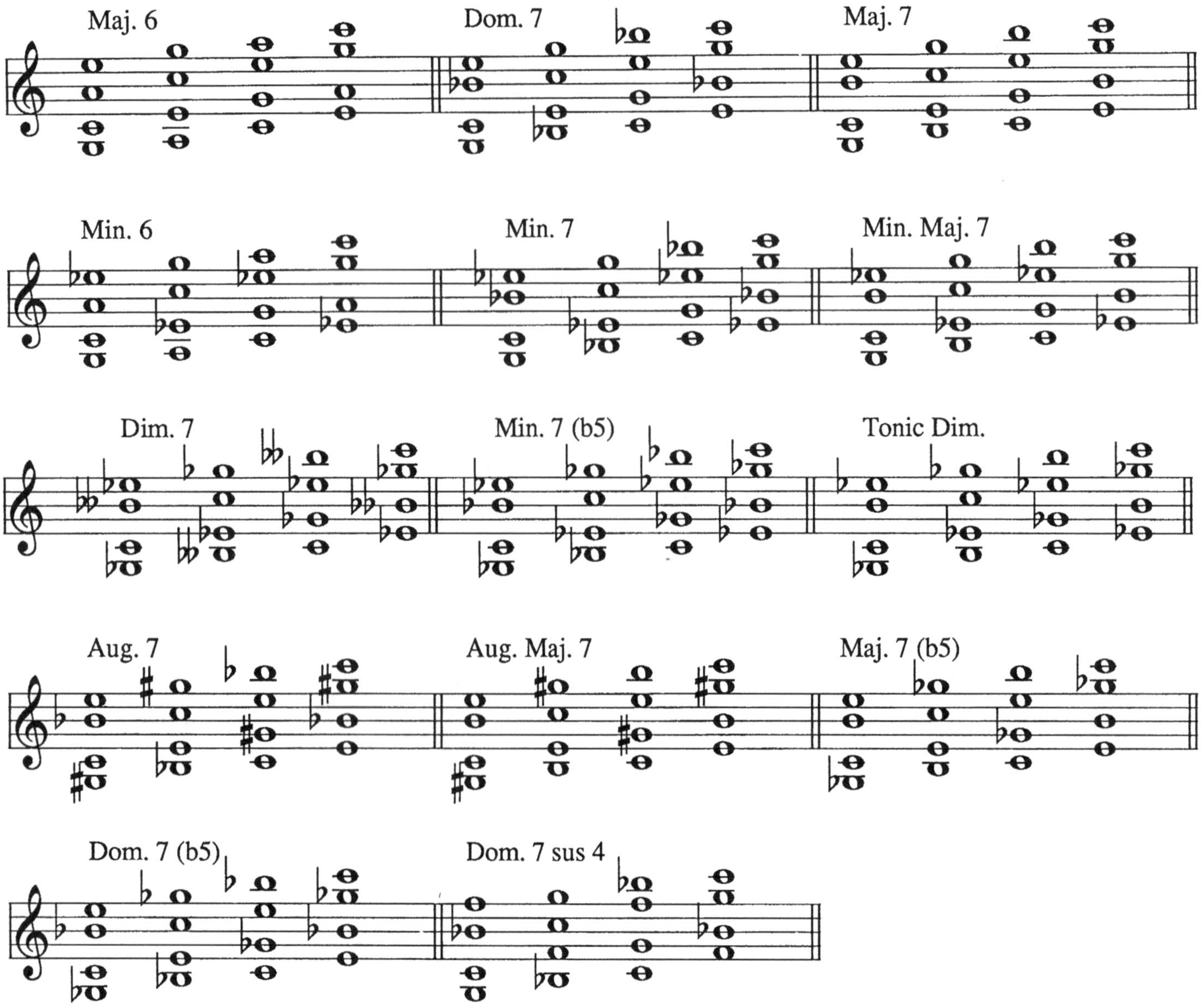
Maj. 6
Dom. 7
Maj. 7
Min. 6
Min. 7
Min. Maj. 7
Dim. 7
Min. 7 (b5)
Tonic Dim.
Aug. 7
Aug. Maj. 7
Maj. 7 (b5)
Dom. 7 (b5)
Dom. 7 sus 4

Intervals, Triads, 7th Chords, Others
Major Scale

Let's take a closer look at the C Major scale.

1. All twelve intervals are contained in a major scale:

minor 2nd	2	(B-C; E-F)
major 2nd	5	(C-D; D-E; F-G; G-A; A-B)
minor 3rds	4	(D-F; E-G; A-C; B-D)
major 3rds	3	(C-E; F-A; G-B)
perfect 4ths	6	(C-F; D-G; E-A; G-C; A-D; B-E)
augmented 4th	1	(F-B)
diminished 5th	1	(B-F)
perfect 5th	6	(C-G; D-A; E-B; F-C; G-D; A-E)
minor 6th	3	(E-C; A-F; B-G)
major 6th	4	(C-A; D-B; F-D; G-E)
minor 7th	5	(D-C; E-D; G-F; A-G; B-A)
major 7th	2	(C-B; F-E)

augmented 4th/diminished 5th (Tritone)	1
minor 2nd/major 7th	2
major 3rd/minor 6th	3
minor 3rd/major 6th	4
major 2nd/minor 7th	5
perfect 4th/perfect 5th	6

3rd/6th family 3 + 4 = 7

2nd/7th family 2 + 5 = 7

4th/5th family 1 + 6 = 7

2. Triads (See Page 48)
The major scale contains:

3 major triads	C F G	I IV V
3 minor triads	D- E- A-	II III VI
1 diminished triad	B°	VII
0 augmented triads		

3. 7th chords (See Page 49)
The major scale contains:

2 major 7th chords	CM7, FM7	I IV
3 minor 7th chords	D-7 E-7 A-7	II III VI
1 dominant 7th chord	G7	V
1 minor 7th (b5) chord	B-7b5	VII

4. 9th, 11th, 13th chords: See hybrid four part voicings, pages 58 to 61.

CM7	9	11	13
D-7	9	11	13
E-7	b9	11	b13
FM7	9	#11	13
G7	9	11	13
A-7	9	11	b13
B-7b5	b9	11	b13

Are these triads?

5. **Quartal Harmony** (fourth voicings) See Page 50.

Three part voicings: P4 + P4 - 5
P4 + TT - 1
TT + P4 - 1

four, five, six- part voicings: see page 50.

Play and identify all triads and cycles.

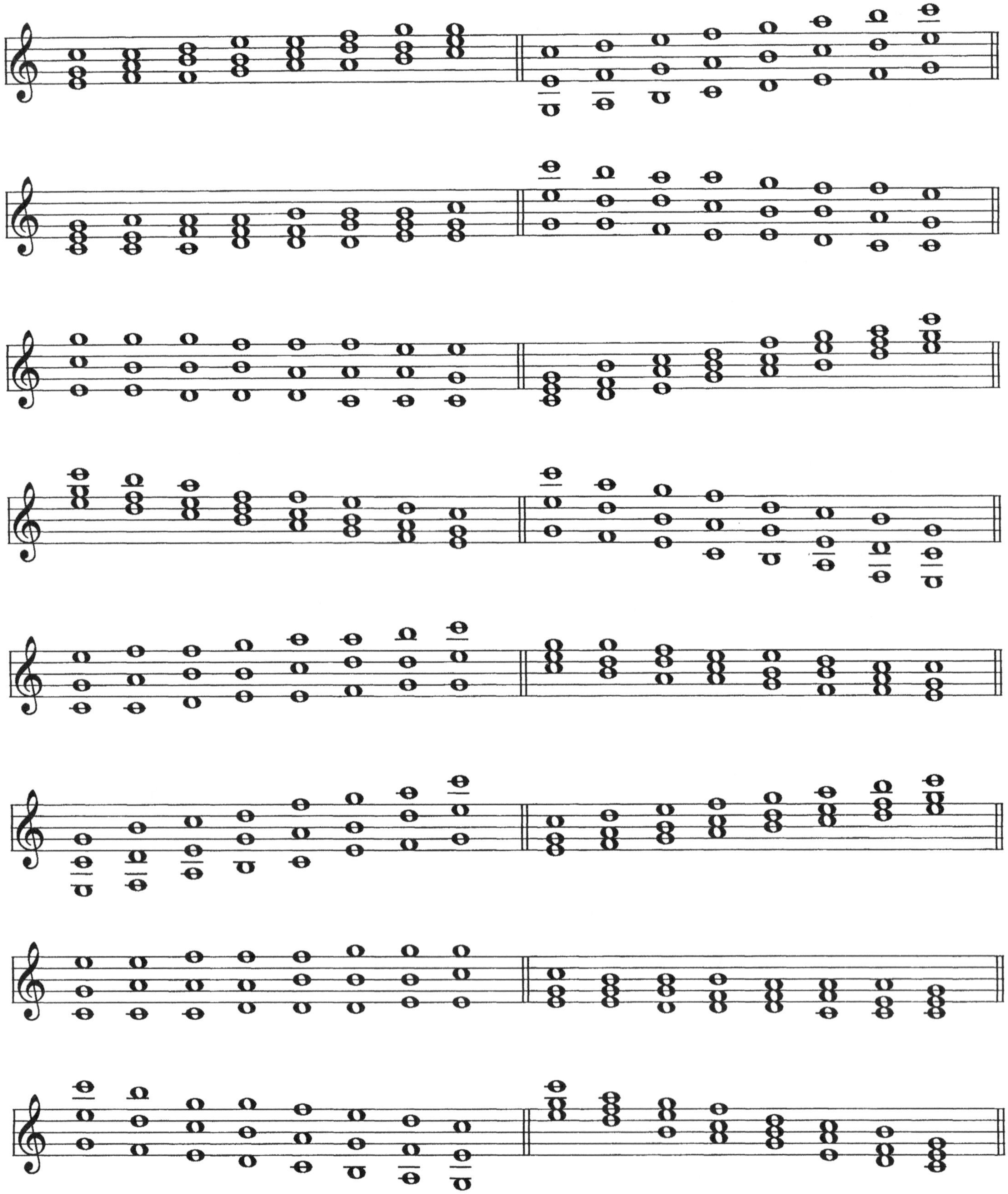

Play and identify all chords and cycles.

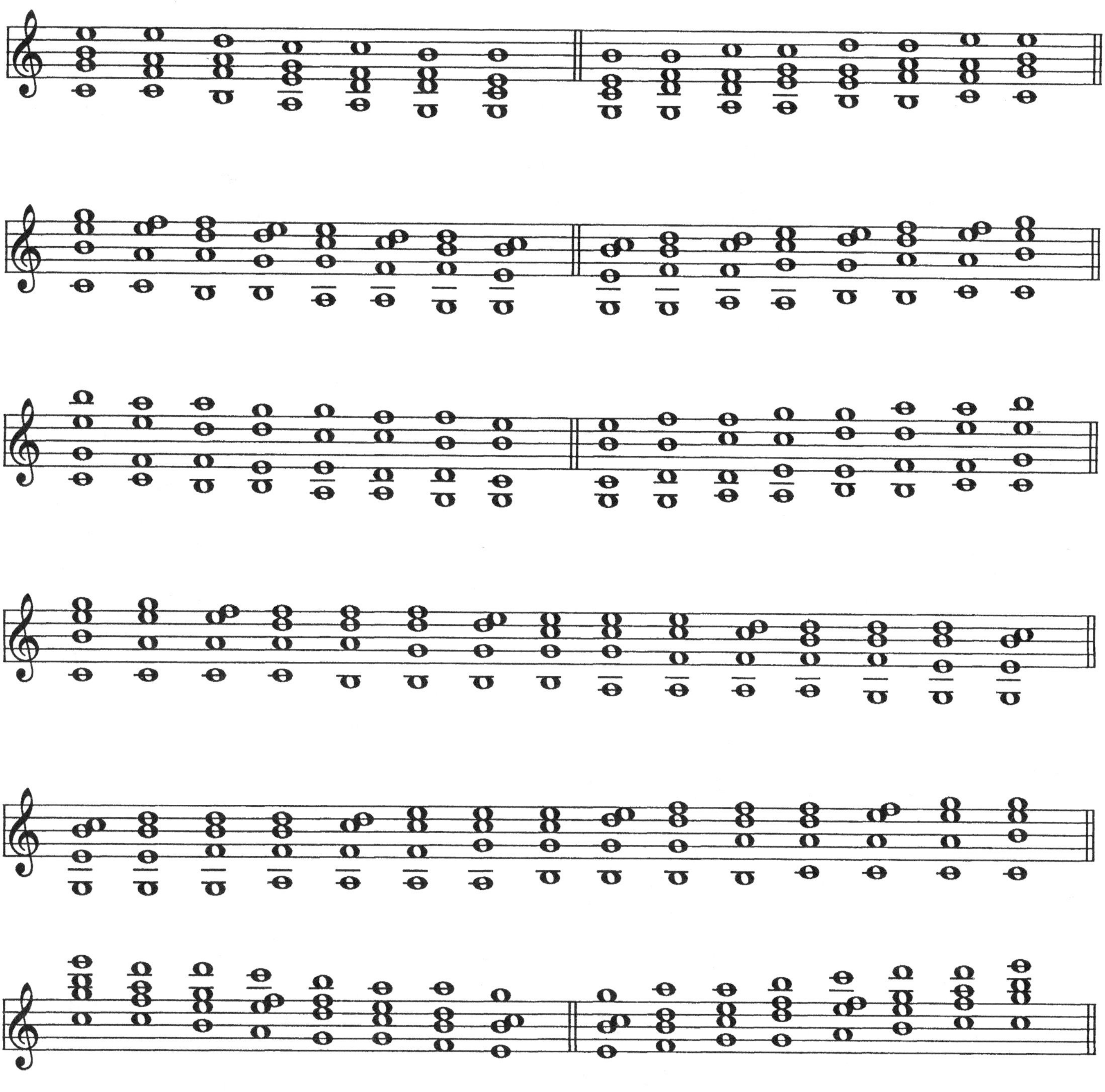

QUARTAL HARMONY
(4th Voicings, C Major Scale)

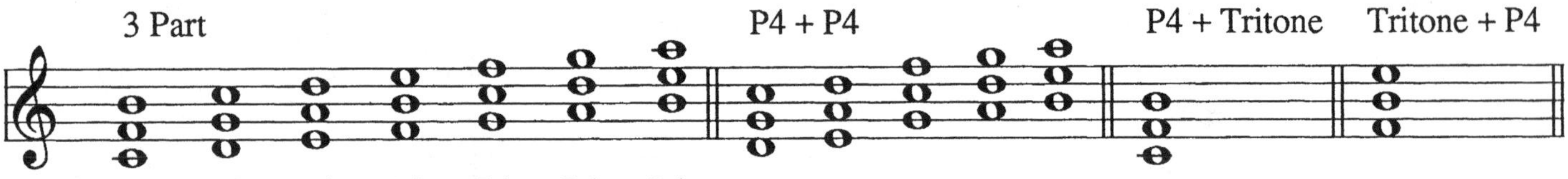
3 Part
P4 + P4
P4 + Tritone
Tritone + P4

TT	P4	P4	P4	P4	P4	P4
P4	P4	P4	TT	P4	P4	P4

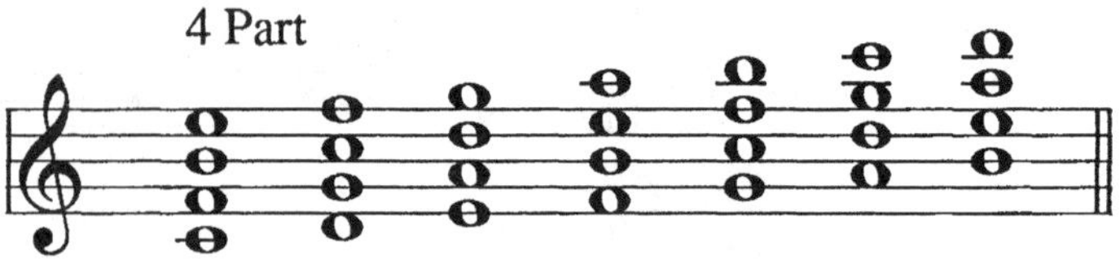
4 Part

P4	P4	P4	P4	TT	P4	P4
TT	P4	P4	P4	P4	P4	P4
P4	P4	P4	TT	P4	P4	P4

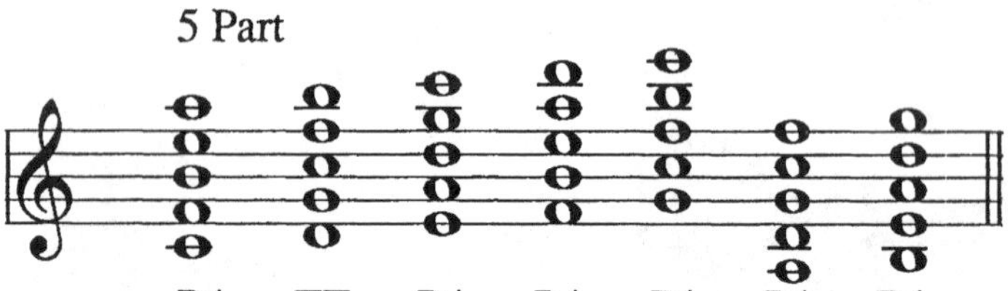
5 Part

P4	TT	P4	P4	P4	P4	P4
P4	P4	P4	P4	TT	P4	P4
TT	P4	P4	P4	P4	P4	P4
P4	P4	P4	TT	P4	P4	P4

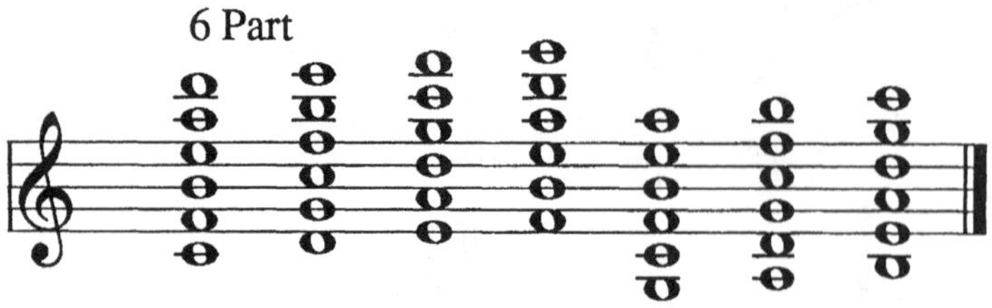
6 Part

P4	P4	P4	P4	P4	TT	P4
P4	TT	P4	P4	P4	P4	P4
P4	P4	P4	P4	TT	P4	P4
TT	P4	P4	P4	P4	P4	P4
P4	P4	P4	TT	P4	P4	P4

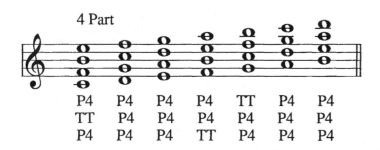

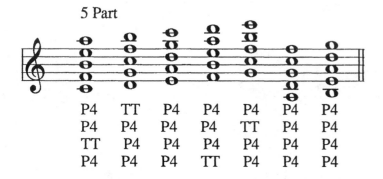

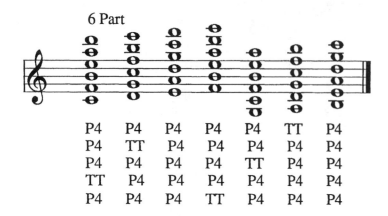

Intervals, Triads, 7th Chords, Others Melodic Minor Scale (Real Melodic Minor or Jazz Minor)

Let's take a closer look at the C melodic minor scale.

1. All twelve intervals are contained in a melodic minor scale:

minor 2nd	2	(B-C; D-Eb)
major 2nd	5	(C-D; Eb-F; F-G; G-A; A-B)
minor 3rd	4	(C-Eb; D-F; A-C; B-D)
major 3rd	3	(Eb-G; F-A; G-B)
perfect 4th	4	(C-F; D-G; G-C; A-D)
augmented 4th	2	(Eb-A; F-B)
diminished 5th	2	(A-Eb; B-F)
perfect 5th	4	(C-G; D-A; F-C; G-D)
minor 6th	3	(G-Eb; A-F; B-G)
major 6th	4	(C-A; D-B; Eb-C; F-D)
minor 7th	5	(D-C; F-Eb; G-F; A-G; B-A)
major 7th	2	(C-B; Eb-D)

augmented 4th/diminished 5th (Tritone)	2
minor 2nd/major 7th	2
major 3rd/minor 6th	3
minor 3rd/major 6th	4
major 2nd/minor 7th	5
perfect 4th/perfect 5th	4

3rd/6th family	3 + 4 =	7
2nd/7th family	2 + 5 =	7
4th/5th family	2 + 4 =	6

The reason this family is one unit short is because of the interval B-Eb, which is a diminished 4th/augmented 5th. Enharmonically, the sound is a major 3rd/minor 6th.

2. Triads

The melodic minor scale contains:

2 major triads	F	G	IV	V
2 minor triads	C-	D-	I	II
2 diminished triads	A°	B°	VI	VII
1 augmented triad	Eb+		III	

3. 7th Chords

The melodic minor scale contains:

2 dominant 7th chords	F7	G7	IV	V
2 minor 7(b5) chords	A-7b5	B-7b5	VI	VII
1 minor 7th chord	D-7		II	
1 minor maj7 chord	C-M7		I	
1 augmented maj7 chord	Eb+M7		III	

4. 9th, 11th, 13th chords See hybrid four-part voicings pages 59 to 61.

C-M7	9	11	13	Are these triads?
D-7	b9	11	13	
Eb+M7	9	#11	13	
F7	9	#11	13	
G7	9	11	b13	
A-7(b5)	9	11	b13	
B-7(b5)	b9	b11	b13	

Notice that the 11th degree of B-7 (b5) is b11. This note is enharmonically the same as 3. Consequently, the mode built on the 7th degree (b) turns out to be B7 altered: 1 b2 b3 b4 b5 b6 b7. This is sometimes called "super Locrian." (It is so "dark" it starts getting "bright"). Functionally, the altered scale is written:

1	b2	#2	3	#4	#5	b7
	b9	#9		#11	b13	
				b5		

You can think:	3 chord tones	1,	3,	b7	and
	4 tensions	b9	#9	b5	#5
				#11	b13

This Super Locrian scale is used against a dominant 7th chord, not a minor 7(b5). Even though the diatonic 7th chord is B-7(b5), the "altered" in alt. dominant means that the 5th and the 9th are altered; which means either raised or lowered (b9, #9, b5, #5). No 9; no 5. This is known as an altesred dominant scale. So, you could change the list of 7th chords to include B7 (b5) and/or B+7 (B7#5). Functionally, you could delete B-7(b5) because the altered scale is not usually used for minor 7(b5).

The Super Locrian or altered dominant scale is also called the diminished - whole tone scale, because it starts out like a diminished scale (B C D Eb; half step - whole step - half step) and ends like a whole tone scale (Eb F G A B; all whole steps).

This is important to keep in mind because all the melodic minor modes have these configurations, but in different areas of each mode.

5. Quartal Harmony (4th voicings)

Three- part voicings:

P4 + P4 - 3	C	F	G
	G	C	D
	D	G	A
P4 + TT - 1	B		
	F		
	C		
TT + P4 - 1	D		
	A		
	Eb		

The other two voicings

Eb		A
B	and	Eb
F		B

are not compatible with the previous five voicings since these two contain the diminished 4th interval (which sounds like a major 3rd). This is not to say that they can't be used at all. It's just that they don't sound "right" in a 3-part harmony context.

QUARTAL HARMONY
(Melodic Minor Scale)

3 Part

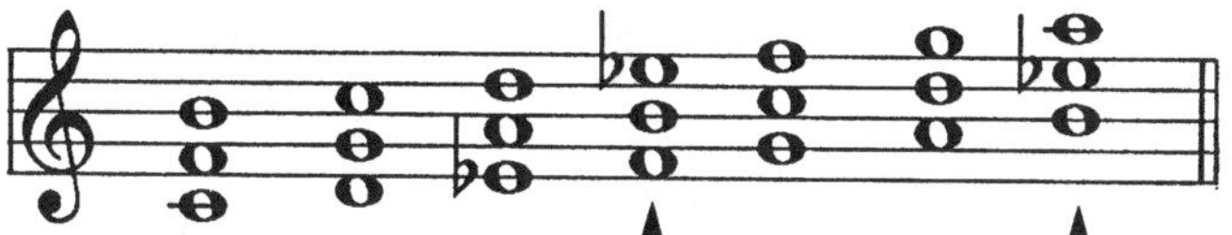

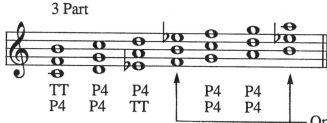

TT	P4	P4		P4	P4	
P4	P4	TT		P4	P4	

Omit because of diminished 4th

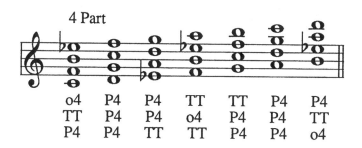

4 Part

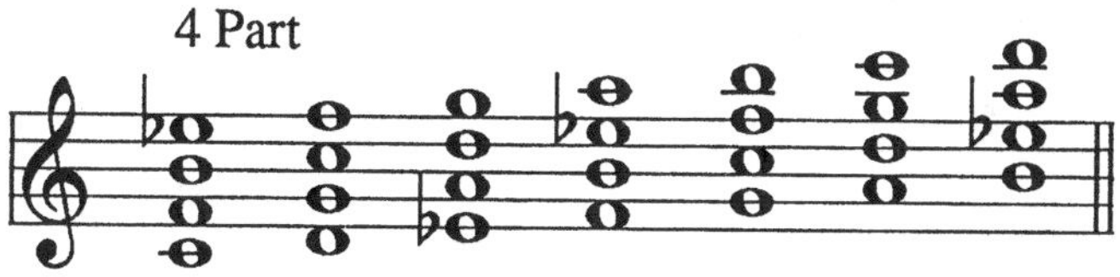

o4	P4	P4	TT	TT	P4	P4
TT	P4	P4	o4	P4	P4	TT
P4	P4	TT	TT	P4	P4	o4

5 Part

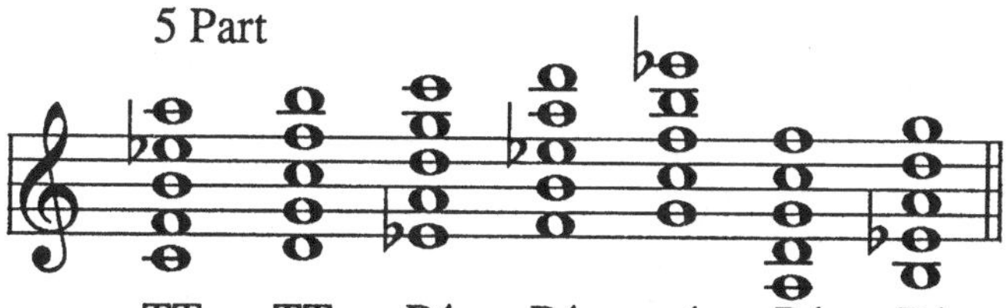

TT	TT	P4	P4	o4	P4	P4
o4	P4	P4	TT	TT	P4	P4
TT	P4	P4	o4	P4	P4	TT
P4	P4	TT	TT	P4	P4	o4

6 Part

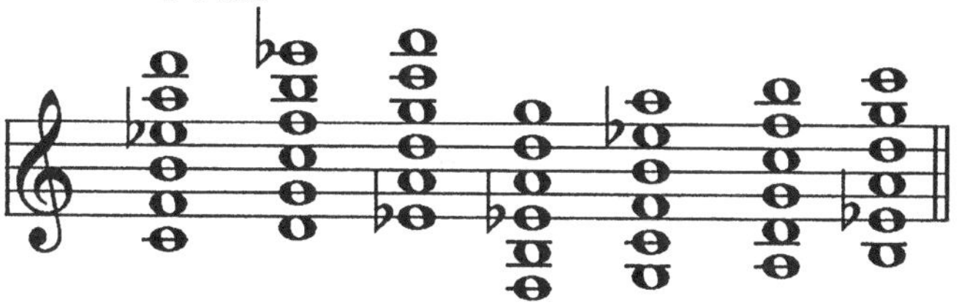

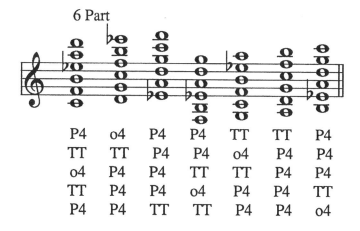

P4	o4	P4	P4	TT	TT	P4
TT	TT	P4	P4	o4	P4	P4
o4	P4	P4	TT	TT	P4	P4
TT	P4	P4	o4	P4	P4	TT
P4	P4	TT	TT	P4	P4	o4

The diminished 4th interval seems to work much better in four, five, and six part 4th voicings. The sound of the major 3rd seems to add a nice quality of "brightness."

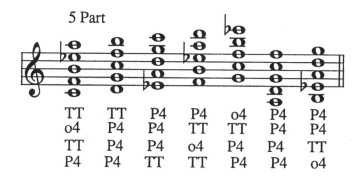

Intervals, Triads, 7th Chords, Others
Harmonic Minor Scale

Let's take a closer look at the C harmonic minor scale.

1. All twelve intervals are contained in a harmonic minor scale:

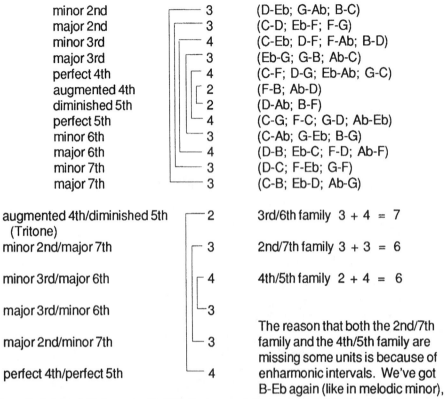

minor 2nd	3	(D-Eb; G-Ab; B-C)
major 2nd	3	(C-D; Eb-F; F-G)
minor 3rd	4	(C-Eb; D-F; F-Ab; B-D)
major 3rd	3	(Eb-G; G-B; Ab-C)
perfect 4th	4	(C-F; D-G; Eb-Ab; G-C)
augmented 4th	2	(F-B; Ab-D)
diminished 5th	2	(D-Ab; B-F)
perfect 5th	4	(C-G; F-C; G-D; Ab-Eb)
minor 6th	3	(C-Ab; G-Eb; B-G)
major 6th	4	(D-B; Eb-C; F-D; Ab-F)
minor 7th	3	(D-C; F-Eb; G-F)
major 7th	3	(C-B; Eb-D; Ab-G)

augmented 4th/diminished 5th (Tritone)	2	3rd/6th family 3 + 4 = 7
minor 2nd/major 7th	3	2nd/7th family 3 + 3 = 6
minor 3rd/major 6th	4	4th/5th family 2 + 4 = 6
major 3rd/minor 6th	3	
major 2nd/minor 7th	3	
perfect 4th/perfect 5th	4	

The reason that both the 2nd/7th family and the 4th/5th family are missing some units is because of enharmonic intervals. We've got B-Eb again (like in melodic minor), which is a diminished 4th/augmented 5th that sounds like a major 3rd/minor 6th. In addition, there is the augmented 2nd/diminished 7th interval, Ab-B (B-Ab), which sounds like a minor 3rd/major 6th. This augmented 2nd interval is really what gives the harmonic minor scale its very distinctive "color". The construction of the major scale and the melodic minor scale involved only half steps and whole steps. In the harmonic minor scale, we've got an interval larger than a whole step between two scale degrees for the first time.

2. Triads

The harmonic minor scale contains:

2 major triads	G Ab	V	VI
2 minor triads	C- F-	I	IV
2 diminished triads	D° B°	II	VII
1 augmented triad	Eb+	III	

3. 7th Chords

The harmonic minor scale contains:

1 major 7th chord	AbM7	VI
1 minor 7th chord	F-7	IV
1 dominant 7th chord	G7	V
1 minor 7(b5) chord	D-7(b5)	II
1 diminished 7th chord	B°7	VII
1 minor major 7th chord	C-M7	I
1 augmented major 7th chord	Eb+M7	III

I think you can see now why it's called the **harmonic** minor scale! (seven different four-part structures). See the hybrid four-part voicings, pages 59 to 61.

4. 9th, 11th, 13th chords

C-M7	9	11	b13	Are these triads?
D-7(b5)	b9	11	13	
Eb+M7	9	11	13	
F-7	9	#11	13	
G7	b9	11	b13	
AbM7	#9	#11	13	
B°7	b9	b11	b13	

Things start to get a bit complicated at this point. Notice that B°7 has a b11. (Enharmonically 3). Also, notice the b13. Since the B°7 already has bb7 (6), this means you get b13, 13, and no 7th! Kind of weird, isn't it? Notice that Eb+M7 has 13. Since Eb+M7 has #5 in it, we get a similar alignment: #5-13. (Although Lydian augmented — third mode of melodic minor — has the same thing, it also has #4, which seems to redeem it somehow. Eb+M7 in C harmonic minor has 11. (Ab) Weird!)

Also notice two other things: F-7 has #11 and AbMajor7 has #9 plus #11. These give very interesting colors that we haven't seen before. We could call the mode built from F a sort of "blues dorian" and the mode built from Ab a sort of "blues Lydian". All of this helps to explain why I suggested that only four harmonic minor modes were really useful. (From 1, 4, 5, 6). From the 2nd degree seems to spoil the sound of the V7(b9) prematurely. From the 3rd degree and 7th degree just seems too "weird". However, this is just my own personal opinion. As always, you must decide for yourself.

5. Quartal Harmony (4th Voicings)

Three-part voicings:					
	B	C	D	F	G
	F	G	Ab	C	D
	C	D	Eb	G	Ab

As in melodic minor, we have the diminished 4th (which sounds like a major 3rd) to consider.

Eb	Ab
B	Eb
F	B (turns out to be an Ab minor triad)

However, since the harmonic minor scale is so interesting harmonically, I think it best to let each person decide what does or doesn't sound good.

QUARTAL HARMONY
(Harmonic Minor Scale)

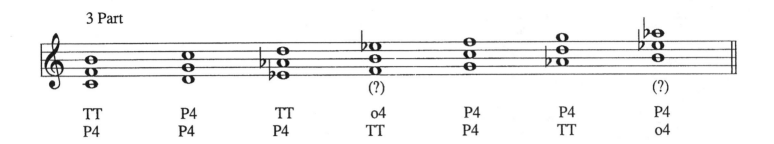

3 Part

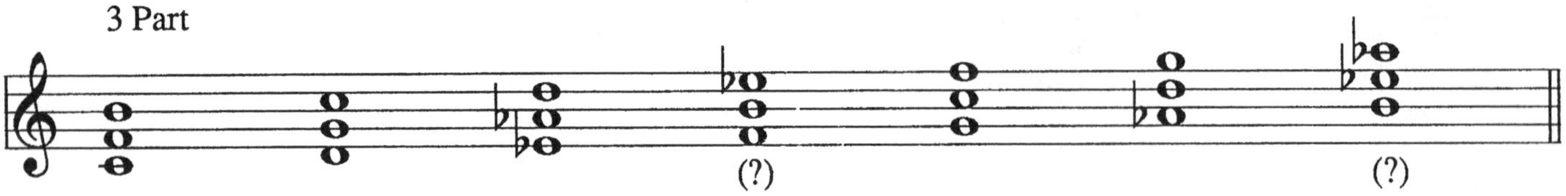
(?)
(?)

TT	P4	TT	o4	P4	P4	P4
P4	P4	P4	TT	P4	TT	o4

4 part

o4	P4	P4	P4	TT	P4	TT
TT	P4	TT	o4	P4	P4	P4
P4	P4	P4	TT	P4	TT	o4

5 part

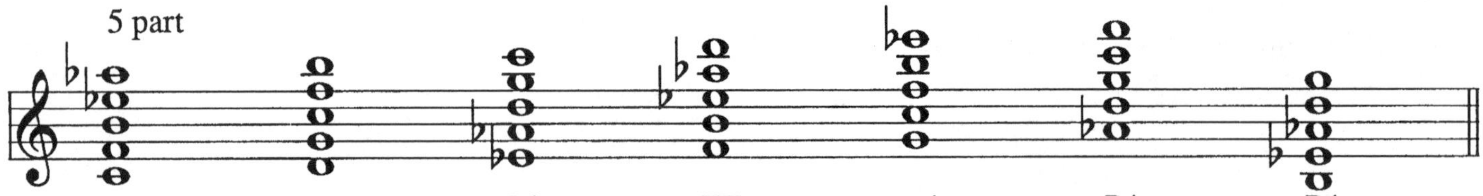

P4	TT	P4	TT	o4	P4	P4
o4	P4	P4	P4	TT	P4	TT
TT	P4	TT	o4	P4	P4	P4
P4	P4	P4	TT	P4	TT	o4

6 Part

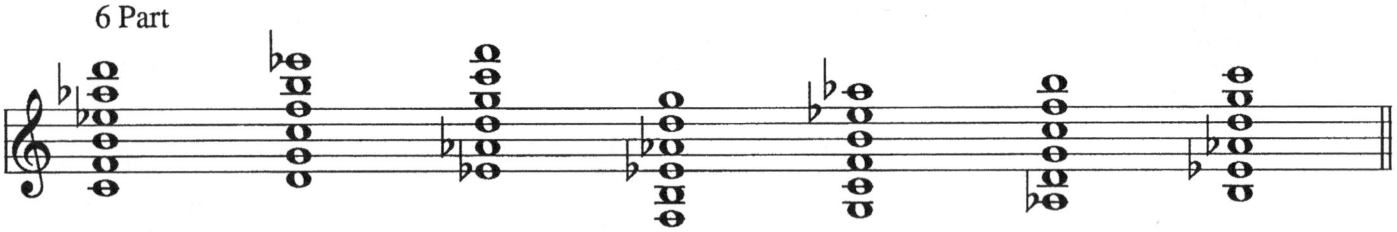

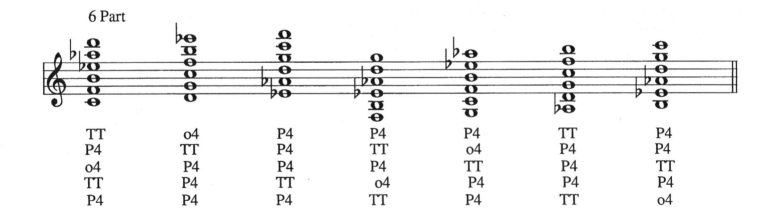

TT	o4	P4	P4	P4	TT	P4
P4	TT	P4	TT	o4	P4	P4
o4	P4	P4	P4	TT	P4	TT
TT	P4	TT	o4	P4	P4	P4
P4	P4	P4	TT	P4	TT	o4

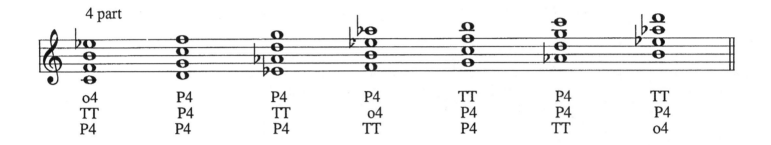

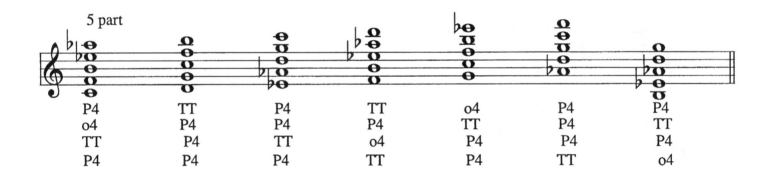

Diatonic Four-part Chords: Part I

In these sets of possibilities, the primary symbol system is the 7th chord terminology while the secondary system is triads over bass notes.

Major (7th chords)

	E-	F	G	A-	B°	C	D-
	C	D	E	F	G	A	B
Cycle 2:	CM7	D-7	E-7	FM7	G7	A-7	B-7b5
	E-	D-	C	B°	A-	G	F
	C	B	A	G	F	E	D
Cycle 7:	CM7	B-7b5	A-7	G7	FM7	E-7	D-7
	E-	G	B°	D-	F	A-	C
	C	E	G	B	D	F	A
Cycle 3:	CM7	E-7	G 7	B-7b5	D-7	FM7	A-7
	E-	C	A-	F	D-	B°	G
	C	A	F	D	B	G	E
Cycle 6:	CM7	A-7	FM7	D-7	B-7b5	G7	E-7
	E-	A-	D-	G	C	F	B°
	C	F	B	E	A	D	G
Cycle 4:	CM7	FM7	B-7b5	E-7	A-7	D-7	G7
	E-	B°	F	C	G	D-	A-
	C	G	D	A	E	B	F
Cycle 5:	CM7	G7	D-7	A-7	E-7	B-7b5	FM7

Melodic Minor (7th chords)

	Eb+	F	G	A°	B°	C-	D-
	C	D	Eb	F	G	A	B
Cycle 2:	C-M7	D-7	Eb+M7	F7	G7	A-7b5	B-7b5
	Eb+	D-	C-	B°	A°	G	F
	C	B	A	G	F	Eb	D
Cycle 7:	C-M7	B-7b5	A-7b5	G7	F7	Eb+M7	D-7
	Eb+	G	B°	D-	F	A°	C-
	C	Eb	G	B	D	F	A
Cycle 3:	C-M7	Eb+M7	G7	B-7b5	D-7	F7	A-7b5
	Eb+	C-	A°	F	D-	B°	G
	C	A	F	D	B	G	Eb
Cycle 6:	C-M7	A-7b5	F7	D-7	B-7b5	G7	Eb+M7
	Eb+	A°	D-	G	C-	F	B°
	C	F	B	Eb	A	D	G
Cycle 4:	C-M7	F7	B-7b5	Eb+M7	A-7b5	D-7	G7
	Eb+	B°	F	C-	G	D-	A°
	C	G	D	A	Eb	B	F
Cycle 5:	C-M7	G7	D-7	A-7b5	Eb+M7	B-7b5	F7

Harmonic Minor (7th chords)

	Eb+	F-	G	Ab	B°	C-	D°
	C	D	Eb	F	G	Ab	B
Cycle 2:	C-M7	D-7b5	Eb+M7	F-7	G7	AbM7	B°7
	Eb+	D°	C-	B°	Ab	G	F-
	C	B	Ab	G	F	Eb	D
Cycle 7:	C-M7	B°7	AbM7	G7	F-7	Eb+M7	D-7b5
	Eb+	G	B°	D°	F-	Ab	C-
	C	Eb	G	B	D	F	Ab
Cycle 3:	C-M7	Eb+M7	G7	B°7	D-7b5	F-7	AbM7
	Eb+	C-	Ab	F-	D°	B°	G
	C	Ab	F	D	B	G	Eb
Cycle 6:	C-M7	AbM7	F-7	D-7b5	B°7	G7	Eb+M7
	Eb+	Ab	D°	G	C-	F-	B°
	C	F	B	Eb	Ab	D	G
Cycle 4:	C-M7	F-7	B°7	Eb+M7	AbM7	D-7b5	G7
	Eb+	B°	F-	C-	G	D°	Ab
	C	G	D	Ab	Eb	B	F
Cycle 5:	C-M7	G7	D-7b5	AbM7	Eb+M7	B°7	F-7

Diatonic four-part Chords: Part II

In these sets, the symbol systems are reversed.

Major 7th chord variation (or hybrid 13th)

	CM7	D-7	E-7	FM7	G7	A-7	B-7b5
	C	D-	E-	F	G	A-	B°
Cycle 2:	B	C	D	E	F	G	A
	CM7	B-7b5	A-7	G7	FM7	E-7	D-7
	C	B°	A-	G	F	E-	D-
Cycle 7:	B	A	G	F	E	D	C
	CM7	E-7	G7	B-7b5	D-7	FM7	A-7
	C	E-	G	B°	D-	F	A-
Cycle 3:	B	D	F	A	C	E	G
	CM7	A-7	FM7	D-7	B-7b5	G7	E-7
	C	A-	F	D-	B°	G	E-
Cycle 6:	B	G	E	C	A	F	D
	CM7	FM7	B-7b5	E-7	A-7	D-7	G7
	C	F	B°	E-	A-	D-	G
Cycle 4:	B	E	A	D	G	C	F
	CM7	G7	D-7	A-7	E-7	B-7b5	FM7
	C	G	D-	A-	E-	B°	F
Cycle 5:	B	F	C	G	D	A	E

Melodic Minor 7th chord variation (or hybrid 13th)

	C-M7	D-7	Eb+M7	F7	G7	A-7b5	B-7b5
	C-	D-	Eb+	F	G	A°	B°
Cycle 2:	B	C	D	Eb	F	G	A
	C-M7	B-7b5	A-7b5	G7	F7	Eb+M7	D-7
	C-	B°	A°	G	F	Eb+	D-
Cycle 7:	B	A	G	F	Eb	D	C
	C-M7	Eb+M7	G7	B-7b5	D-7	F7	A-7b5
	C-	Eb+	G	B°	D-	F	A°
Cycle 3:	B	D	F	A	C	Eb	G
	C-M7	A-7b5	F7	D-7	B-7b5	G7	Eb+M7
	C-	A°	F	D-	B°	G	Eb+
Cycle 6:	B	G	Eb	C	A	F	D
	C-M7	F7	B-7b5	Eb+M7	A-7b5	D-7	G7
	C-	F	B°	Eb+	A°	D-	G
Cycle 4:	B	Eb	A	D	G	C	F
	C-M7	G7	D-7	A-7b5	Eb+M7	B-7b5	F7
	C-	G	D-	A°	Eb+	B°	F
Cycle 5:	B	F	C	G	D	A	Eb

Harmonic Minor 7th chord variation (or hybrid 13th)

	C-M7	D-7b5	Eb+M7	F-7	G7	AbM7	B°7
	C-	D°	Eb+	F-	G	Ab	B°
Cycle 2:	B	C	D	Eb	F	G	Ab
	C-M7	B°7	AbM7	G7	F-7	Eb+M7	D-7b5
	C-	B°	Ab	G	F-	Eb+	D°
Cycle 7:	B	Ab	G	F	Eb	D	C
	C-M7	Eb+M7	G7	B°7	D-7b5	F-7	AbM7
	C-	Eb+	G	B°	D°	F-	Ab
Cycle 3:	B	D	F	Ab	C	Eb	G
	C-M7	AbM7	F-7	D-7b5	B°7	G7	Eb+M7
	C-	Ab	F-	D°	B°	G	Eb+
Cycle 6:	B	G	Eb	C	Ab	F	D
	C-M7	F-7	B°7	Eb+M7	AbM7	D-7b5	G7
	C-	F-	B°	Eb+	Ab	D°	G
Cycle 4:	B	Eb	Ab	D	G	C	F
	C-M7	G7	D-7b5	AbM7	Eb+M7	B°7	F-7
	C-	G	D°	Ab	Eb+	B°	F-
Cycle 5:	B	F	C	G	D	Ab	Eb

Diatonic 4-part Chords: Part III

In these sets, there is no succint 7th chord terminology system, so the sole system is triads over bass notes.

Major (hybrid 9th)

	G	A-	B°	C	D-	E-	F
Cycle 2:	C	D	E	F	G	A	B
	G	F	E-	D-	C	B°	A-
Cycle 7:	C	B	A	G	F	E	D
	G	B°	D-	F	A-	C	E-
Cycle 3:	C	E	G	B	D	F	A
	G	E-	C	A-	F	D-	B°
Cycle 6:	C	A	F	D	B	G	E
	G	C	F	B°	E-	A-	D-
Cycle 4:	C	F	B	E	A	D	G
	G	D-	A-	E-	B°	F	C
Cycle 5:	C	G	D	A	E	B	F

Melodic Minor (hybrid 9th)

	G	A°	B°	C-	D-	Eb+	F
Cycle 2:	C	D	Eb	F	G	A	B
	G	F	Eb+	D-	C-	B°	A°
Cycle 7:	C	B	A	G	F	Eb	D
	G	B°	D-	F	A°	C-	Eb+
Cycle 3:	C	Eb	G	B	D	F	A
	G	Eb+	C-	A°	F	D-	B°
Cycle 6:	C	A	F	D	B	G	Eb
	G	C-	F	B°	Eb+	A°	D-
Cycle 4:	C	F	B	Eb	A	D	G
	G	D-	A°	Eb+	B°	F	C-
Cycle 5:	C	G	D	A	Eb	B	F

Harmonic Minor (hybrid 9th)

	G	Ab	B°	C-	D°	Eb+	F-
Cycle 2:	C	D	Eb	F	G	Ab	B
	G	F-	Eb+	D°	C-	B°	Ab
Cycle 7:	C	B	Ab	G	F	Eb	D
	G	B°	D°	F-	Ab	C-	Eb+
Cycle 3:	C	Eb	G	B	D	F	Ab
	G	Eb+	C-	Ab	F-	D°	B°
Cycle 6:	C	Ab	F	D	B	G	Eb
	G	C-	F-	B°	Eb+	Ab	D°
Cycle 4:	C	F	B	Eb	Ab	D	G
	G	D°	Ab	Eb+	B°	F-	C-
Cycle 5:	C	G	D	Ab	Eb	B	F

Diatonic 4-part Chords: Part IV

In these sets there is no succint 7th chord terminology system, so the sole system is triads over bass notes.

Major (hybrid 11th)

	B°	C	D-	E-	F	G	A-
Cycle 2:	C	D	E	F	G	A	B
	B°	A-	G	F	E-	D-	C
Cycle 7:	C	B	A	G	F	E	D
	B°	D-	F	A-	C	E-	G
Cycle 3:	C	E	G	B	D	F	A
	B°	G	E-	C	A-	F	D-
Cycle 6:	C	A	F	D	B	G	E
	B°	E-	A-	D-	G	C	F
Cycle 4:	C	F	B	E	A	D	G
	B°	F	C	G	D-	A-	E-
Cycle 5:	C	G	D	A	E	B	F

Melodic Minor (hybrid 11th)

	B°	C-	D-	Eb+	F	G	A°
Cycle 2:	C	D	Eb	F	G	A	B
	B°	A°	G	F	Eb+	D-	C-
Cycle 7:	C	B	A	G	F	Eb	D
	B°	D-	F	A°	C-	Eb+	G
Cycle 3:	C	Eb	G	B	D	F	A
	B°	G	Eb+	C-	A°	F	D-
Cycle 6:	C	A	F	D	B	G	Eb
	B°	Eb+	A°	D-	G	C-	F
Cycle 4:	C	F	B	Eb	A	D	G
	B°	F	C-	G	D-	A°	Eb+
Cycle 5:	C	G	D	A	Eb	B	F

Harmonic Minor (hybrid 11th)

	B°	C-	D°	Eb+	F-	G	Ab
Cycle 2:	C	D	Eb	F	G	Ab	B
	B°	Ab	G	F-	Eb+	D°	C-
Cycle 7:	C	B	Ab	G	F	Eb	D
	B°	D°	F-	Ab	C-	Eb+	G
Cycle 3:	C	Eb	G	B	D	F	Ab
	B°	G	Eb+	C-	Ab	F-	D°
Cycle 6:	C	Ab	F	D	B	G	Eb
	B°	Eb+	Ab	D°	G	C-	F-
Cycle 4:	C	F	B	Eb	Ab	D	G
	B°	F-	C-	G	D°	Ab	Eb+
Cycle 5:	C	G	D	Ab	Eb	B	F

Modes; Chord-scales: II

When it comes to chord-scale relationships, a lot of different people will tell you a lot of different things. Most of the time, there's some truth to what anyone might tell you. However, you need to watch out for any tendency to think that "there must be *one* way that's the best." There isn't.

Any sytem of chord-scale relationships is bound to have certain advantages *as well as* certain disadvantages. Consequently, I'd advise anyone to find out as much as possible about many different approaches.

Initially, the two most important approaches are derivative and parallel (as we've indicated before). Derivative has the advantage of relying on relatively few "master scales," which would include the major scale, the real melodic minor scale, the harmonic minor scale, the symetrical diminished scale, the whole tone scale, the pentatonic scale, etc. The complexity of this approach involves the fact that you need to learn many different relationships of how the "master scale" relates to the chord type. Examples: chord symbol is F Lydian. Think major scale built on the fifth degree (C major scale).

Chord symbol is G7 altered. Think melodic minor scale built from b9 (Ab melodic minor scale).

Chord symbol is A7(b9)b13. Think harmonic minor scale built from the root of where this dominant chord would tend to resolve (D harmonic minor scale).

The Parallel approach starts out with all the complexity because in the beginning you have to learn seven different modes from the major scale, seven modes from the melodic minor, seven modes from the harmonic minor, etc. As difficult as this may seem, it does have the distinct advantage of a consistent understanding of note relationships from the roots of the chords. Consequently, this approach (parallel) is usually understood to be especially important and useful for musicians who play chords. This way,we know not only the notes that are available, but also their relationship to the chord type in terms of chord-tones and tensions.

In some situations, it's fairly obvious that derivative is quicker than parallel or vice versa. For instance, if the chord symbol is Gb Lydian, derivative thinking might be too slow: "What is the major scale of which Gb is the 4th degree? Let's see, do I go up a fifth or down a fifth?" The chord might be over before you figure it out. Whereas, if you know that Lydian means a major scale with the 4th degree raised a half step, you can get to the notes right away. So, in this situation, it would appear that parallel thinking is quicker than derivative.

On the other hand, if the chord symbol is A#-7(b5), parallel thinking would be very cumbersome, to put it mildly: "Let's see, Minor 7(b5) is Locrian. All I have to do is take an A# major scale (A# B# Cx D# E# Fx Gx A#) and flat the 2nd, the 3rd, the 5th, the 6th and the 7th." (By the time you figured it out, the whole tune could be over!) Derivative thinking would be much faster: "Minor 7(b5) is Locrian. Major scale up a half step. Oh! It's the notes of a B major scale from the 7th degree, A#!"

In addition to derivative and parallel, there are other ways of looking at chord-scale relationships. Probably the most well-known of alternative chord-scale relationships would be the Lydian Chromatic Concept. (It is beyond the scope of this essay to go into any depth on the details of the Lydian Chromatic Concept. Anyone interested should see George Russell's book, **The Lydian Chromatic Concept of Tonal Organization**). One appealing feature of the L. C. C. is that it is a complete and consistent system within itself. One less apppealing feature is that it can tend to be confusing to someone who doesn't already have a strong background in both derivative and parallel thinking. Like any other approach, the L. C. C. has it's own distinct advantages and disadvantages. I would call the L. C. C. a hybrid derivative approach because, like derivative, you don't have to learn all the modes that you have to learn in parallel. You *do* need to learn particular scales, in different relationships to chord-types, but the "parent scales" are somewhat different than in normal derivative thinking.

I personally think that the most valuable aspect of the L.C.C. has to do with the way that the author "looked at the overview." The way that he chose to organize it was one of several possibilities. But the fact that someone could look this way is quite valuable, I think. There are examples of L.C.C. thinking that I've found to be very useful. You'll find some of them in this present volume. Again, I must add that my own feeling is that any system has certain "traps" built into it by virtue of being a "system." On the other hand, to disregard the benefits and valuable aspects of someone's work just because it's a system would be silly. So, my advice would be to check it out if you're interested, and take from it what makes sense for you.

There is one other approach to chord-scale relationships that needs to be mentioned: Common-tone thinking. (To my knowledge there has been no organized approach or method to this kind of thinking, even though many players use it from time to time.) As you might guess, it has to do with common tones. In its most simple form, it could be expressed as: "What stays the same? And what changes?" It works in progressions of chords that have a common tone. For purposes of demonstration, let's take a couple of progressions and show all four ways of chord-scale thinking followed by a theme that has been moved around to fit each of the four approaches.

Ex. No. 1

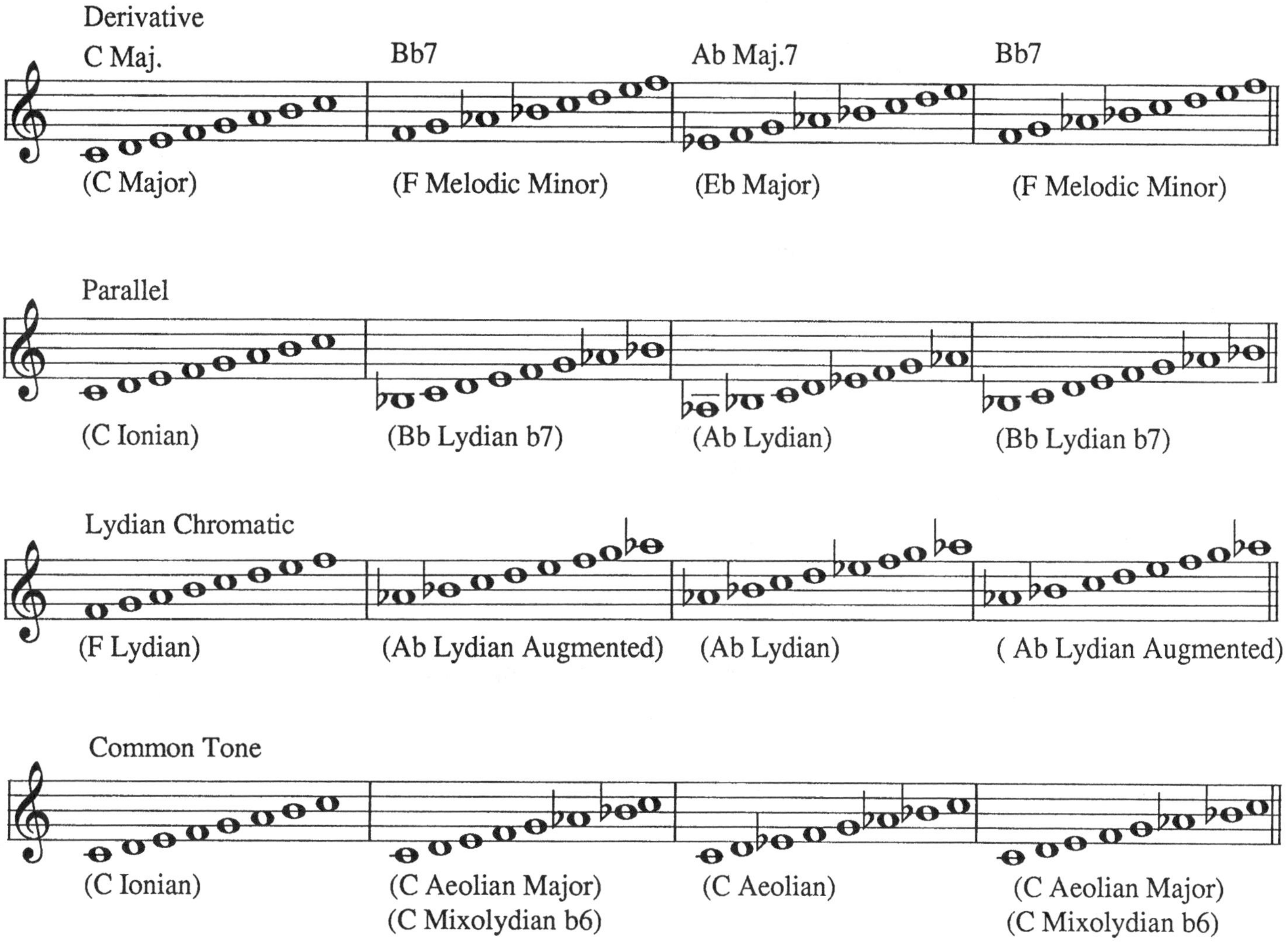

Derivative
C Maj.
Bb7
Ab Maj.7
Bb7
(C Major)
(F Melodic Minor)
(Eb Major)
(F Melodic Minor)
Parallel
(C Ionian)
(Bb Lydian b7)
(Ab Lydian)
(Bb Lydian b7)
Lydian Chromatic
(F Lydian)
(Ab Lydian Augmented)
(Ab Lydian)
(Ab Lydian Augmented)
Common Tone
(C Ionian)
(C Aeolian Major)
(C Mixolydian b6)
(C Aeolian)
(C Aeolian Major)
(C Mixolydian b6)

Theme: 7 1 2 3 4 6 5

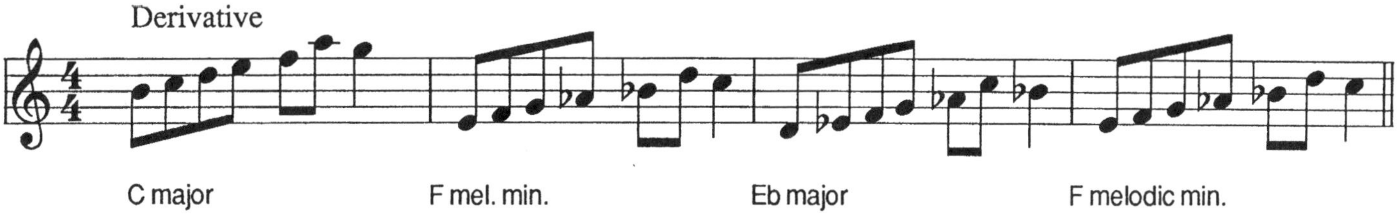

Derivative
C major
F mel. min.
Eb major
F melodic min.

Parallel

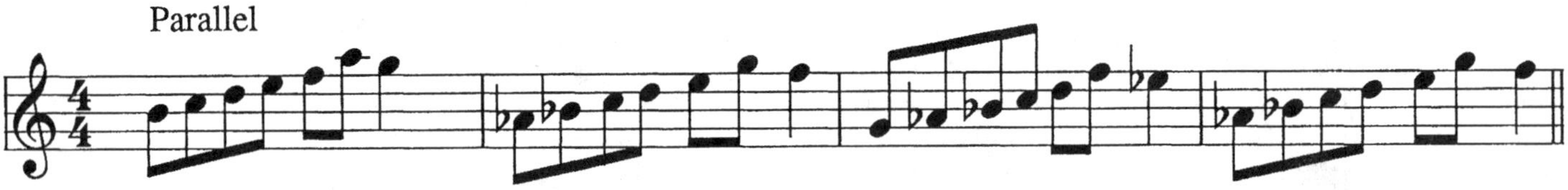

C Ionian | Bb Lyd.b7 | Ab Lyd. | Bb Lyd. b7

Lydian Chromatic

F Lydian | Ab Lyd. aug. | Ab Lyd. | Ab Lyd. aug.

Common Tone

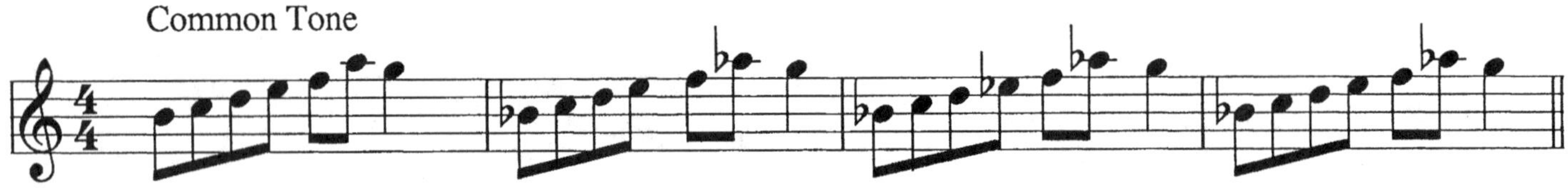

C Ionian | C Aeolian maj. C Mixo. b6 | C Aeolian | C Aeolian maj. C Mixo. b6

Notice that in each of the four approaches, you are still using exactly the same notes for each chord. But I think that if you played through the progression a number of times using each of the four approaches, you would come up with different results.

Observations for Example No. 1

- Derivative is probably the easiest, but you "jump around" some.
- With parallel you tend to shape your ideas the same way the chords move.
- With Lydian Chromatic Concept, thinking F Lydian for C maj. 7 is a bit tricky for most people. On the other hand, the rest of the progression turns out to be strung together in common-tone thinking.
- With common-tone thinking, you can stay right where you are and play without moving around a lot because it's easy to see "what's the same? And what changes?"

Ex. No. 2

Derivative
C Maj. 7 #11
A7 Alt.
D-7 (b5) ♮9
G7 Alt.
(G Major)
(Bb Melodic Minor)
(F Melodic Minor)
(Ab Melodic Minor)

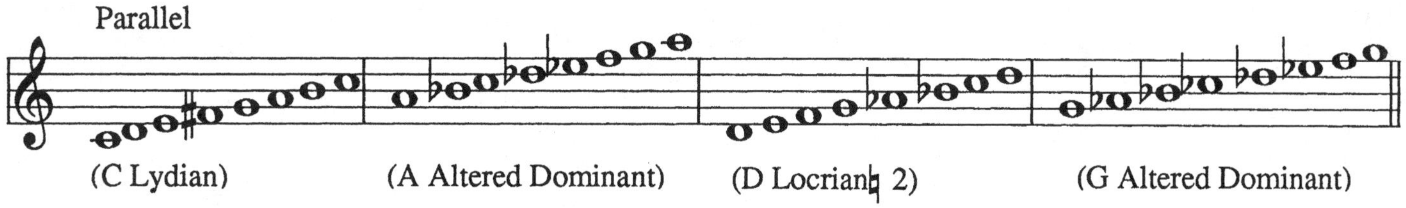
Parallel
(C Lydian)
(A Altered Dominant)
(D Locrian ♮ 2)
(G Altered Dominant)

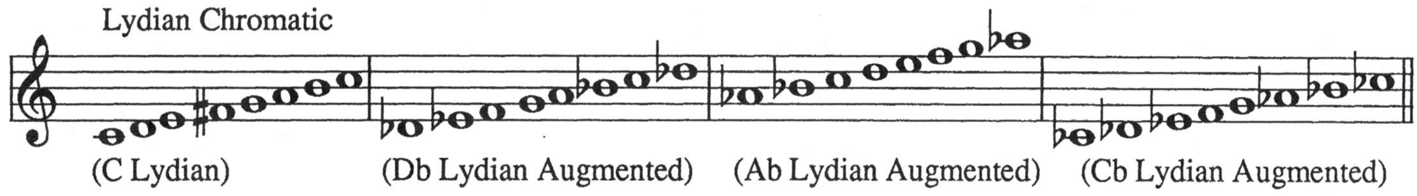
Lydian Chromatic
(C Lydian)
(Db Lydian Augmented)
(Ab Lydian Augmented)
(Cb Lydian Augmented)

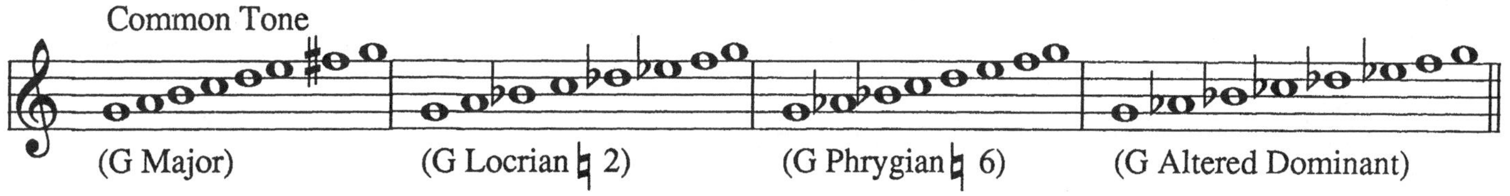
Common Tone
(G Major)
(G Locrian ♮ 2)
(G Phrygian ♮ 6)
(G Altered Dominant)

Theme: 3 1 2 5 4 7 6

Derivative
G major
Bb mel. min.
F mel. min.
Ab mel. min.

Parallel
C Lydian
A7 alt.
D Locrian ♮ 2
G7 alt.

Lydian Chromatic

C Lydian | Db Lyd. aug. | Ab Lyd. aug. | Cb Lyd. aug.

Common Tone

G major | G Locrian 2 | G Phry. 6 | G alt.

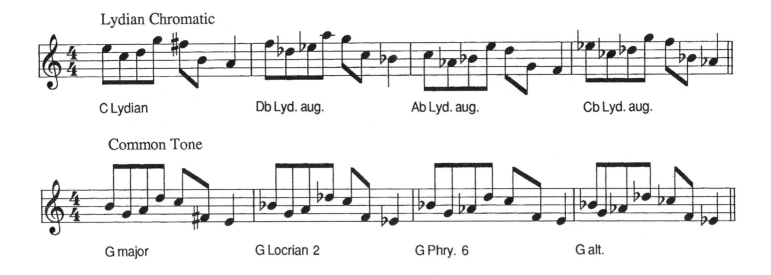

Observations for Example No. 2

- After playing the four variations of the theme, you might be tempted to experiment with skipping from one measure of one approach to another measure of another approach. I certainly hope so!
- You might even see the possibility of transposing the theme to get even more variations than were given. If so, go for it! (Themes and variations are a very important part of improvising.)
- You might experiment with your own seven- note themes. (If you run out of ideas, you could use a telephone book for source material).
- You might experiment with themes of less than seven notes (or more).

Afterthoughts:

Again, no single approach is "the best." But each approach has definite uses. Each is valuable. Each is worthwhile exploring.

Derivative: Accessible; very good for "an overview."

Parallel: Important harmonically; very good for "specifics."

Lydian Chromatic: Less accessible than normal derivative; very good for "another overview" (could lead to even more "overviews)."

Common-tone: Uniquely different from previous 3 approaches; more like an "underview" than an "overview."

Chord Type	Mode(s)
Major 7th	Ionian; Lydian; (Lydian#2); (Lydian augmented)
Minor 7th	Dorian; Phrygian; Aeolian; (Dorian#4)
Minor major 7th	melodic minor; harmonic minor
Minor 7(b5)	Locrian; Locrian ♮2
Dominant 7th	Mixolydian; Lydian b7; Aeolian major; altered dominant; Phrygian major; Dorian b2; whole-tone; symmetrical diminished (1/2, 1, 1/2, 1, 1/2, 1, 1/2, 1)
Major 7 #5	Lydian augmented

Process

I'd like to show you something that I think is interesting. After deciding to demonstrate how the Major 7th, Maj. 7(b5) and Maj. 7(#5) chords can be used as substitutes for other chords, I was listing for myself the possible functions of CMaj. 7. I came up with six possible uses:

1. C Maj. 7

2. D7 sus 4(9,13)

3. D-11 (in Dorian only)

4. F M7(#11)

5. A-7

6. B7sus4 (#5 , b9)

Then I figured it would be a good idea to show the use of C Major 7th for each of the six chords in progressions where the chords occurred in context. So I wrote six progressions of three (or four) chords. Then, I wrote several more versions of each of the six functions using different voicings of the C maj. 7 chord. (The progressions were usually II V I or some variation of it.) I compiled all the material and wrote it out on paper (which follows).

Then I wondered if it would be possible to string these small harmonic fragments together to make a larger progression. (The trick would be to use each and every fragment, but only once !) After much experimenting, I finally figured out a way to do it. I admit I did take some "artistic liberties" when I needed, but that's okay to do. Then I wrote it out on paper (which follows).

> If you write something like this that works,
> you call it a "chord progression".
> If it not only works but really sounds good to you,
> you call it a "harmonic continuity!"

In this case, the harmonic continuity came first. Then, I simplified it to write the progression (the changes) which follows.

Play through and study all of the following pages:

Uses of C Major

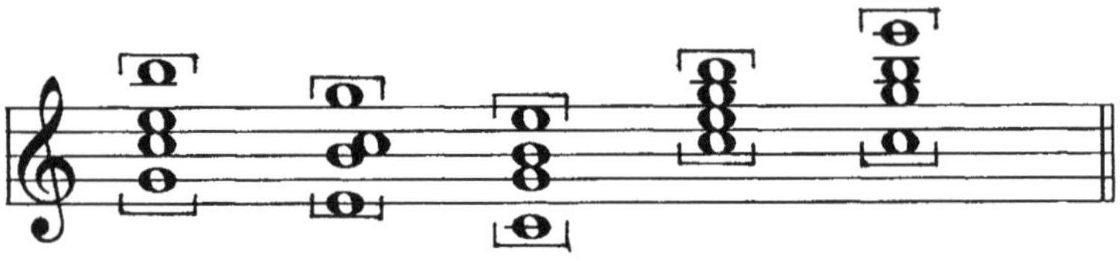

As C Maj.7

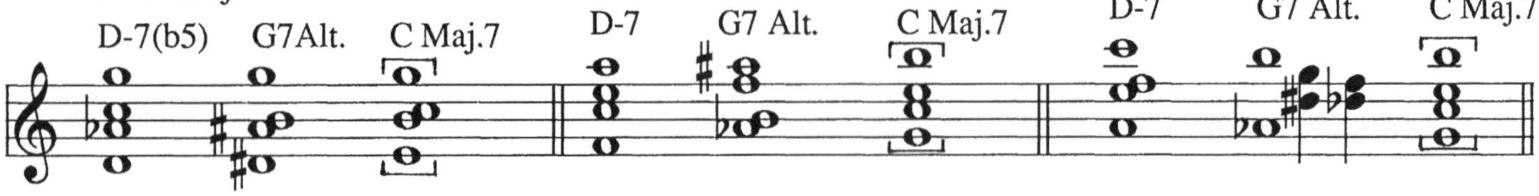
D-7(b5)
G7Alt.
C Maj.7
D-7
G7 Alt.
C Maj.7
D-7
G7 Alt.
C Maj.7

As D7 Sus 4 (9,13)

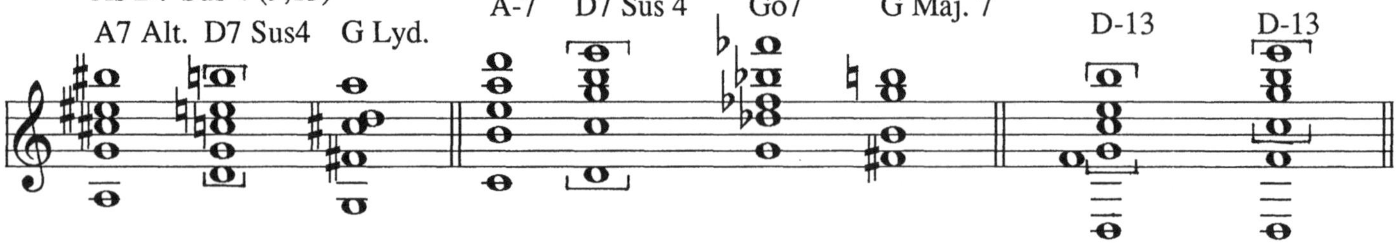
A7 Alt.
D7 Sus4
G Lyd.
A-7
D7 Sus 4
Go7
G Maj. 7
As D Dorian
D-13
D-13

As F Lydian

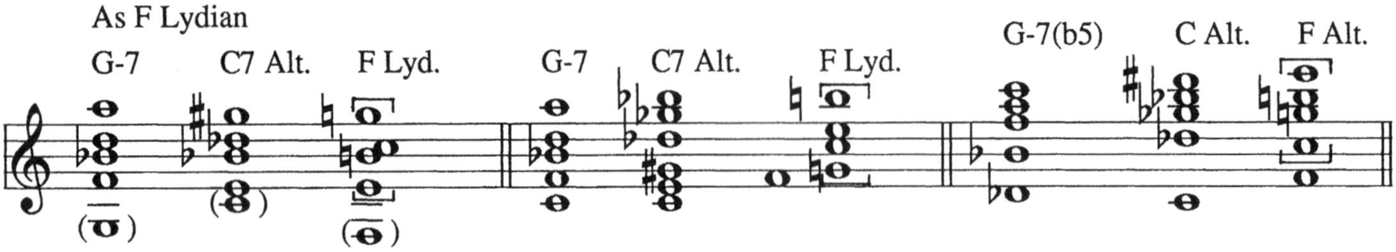
G-7
C7 Alt.
F Lyd.
G-7
C7 Alt.
F Lyd.
G-7(b5)
C Alt.
F Alt.

As B+7 Sus 4 b9

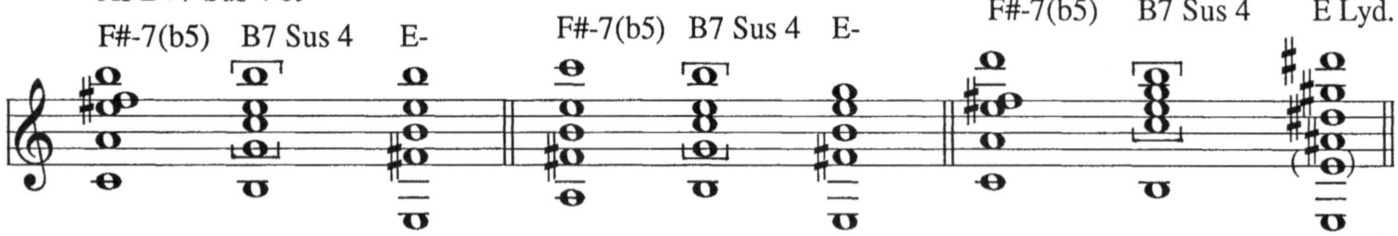
F#-7(b5)
B7 Sus 4
E-
F#-7(b5)
B7 Sus 4
E-
F#-7(b5)
B7 Sus 4
E Lyd.

As A-7

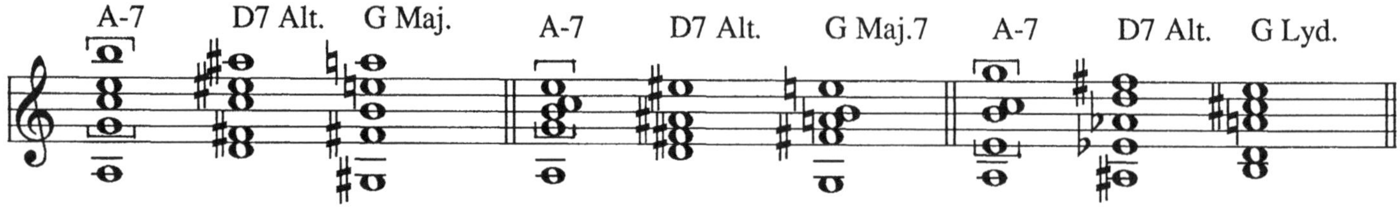
A-7
D7 Alt.
G Maj.
A-7
D7 Alt.
G Maj.7
A-7
D7 Alt.
G Lyd.

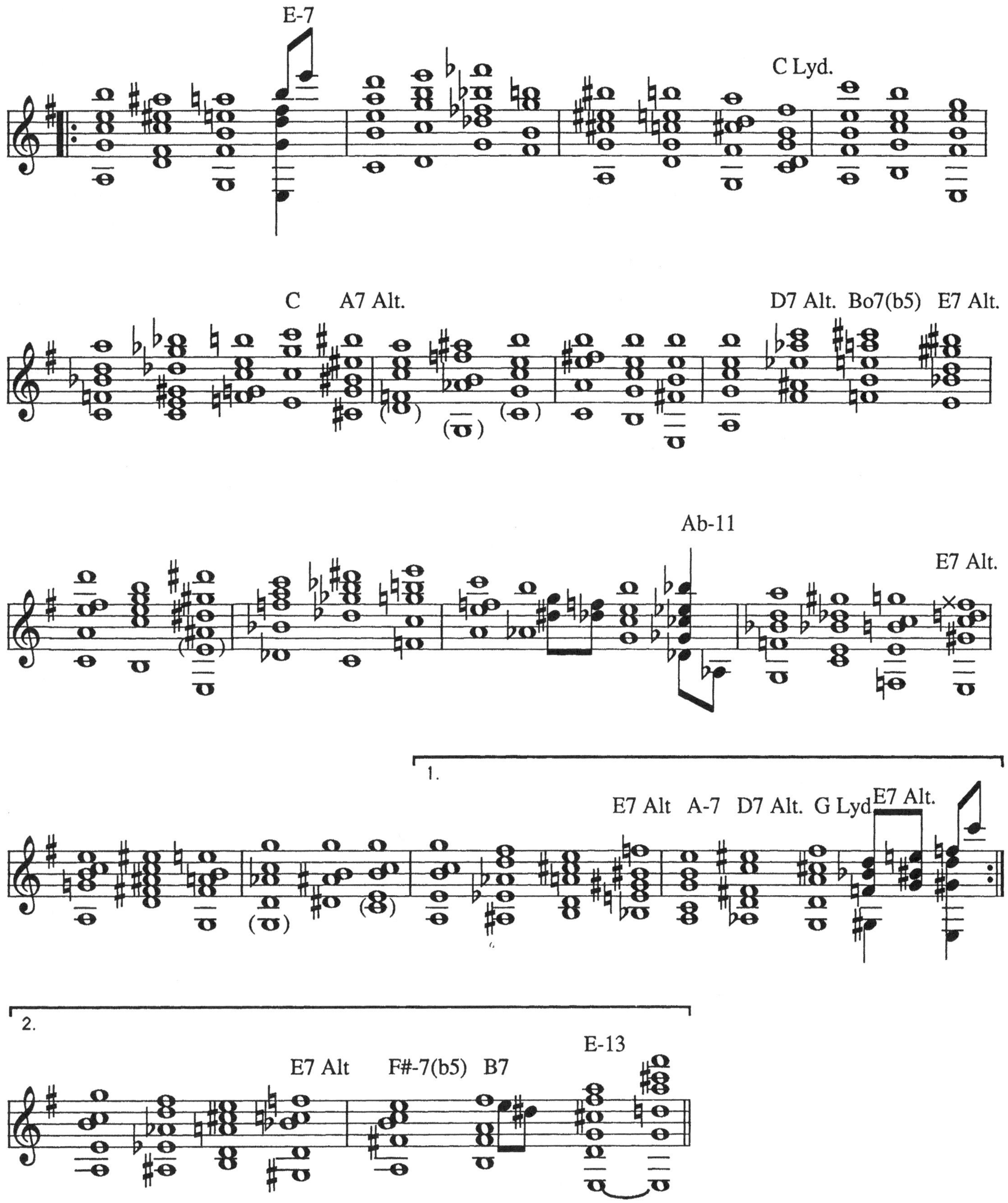
E-7
C Lyd.
C
A7 Alt.
D7 Alt.
Bo7(b5)
E7 Alt.
Ab-11
E7 Alt.
1.
E7 Alt
A-7
D7 Alt.
G Lyd
E7 Alt.
2.
E7 Alt
F#-7(b5)
B7
E-13

Chord Progression

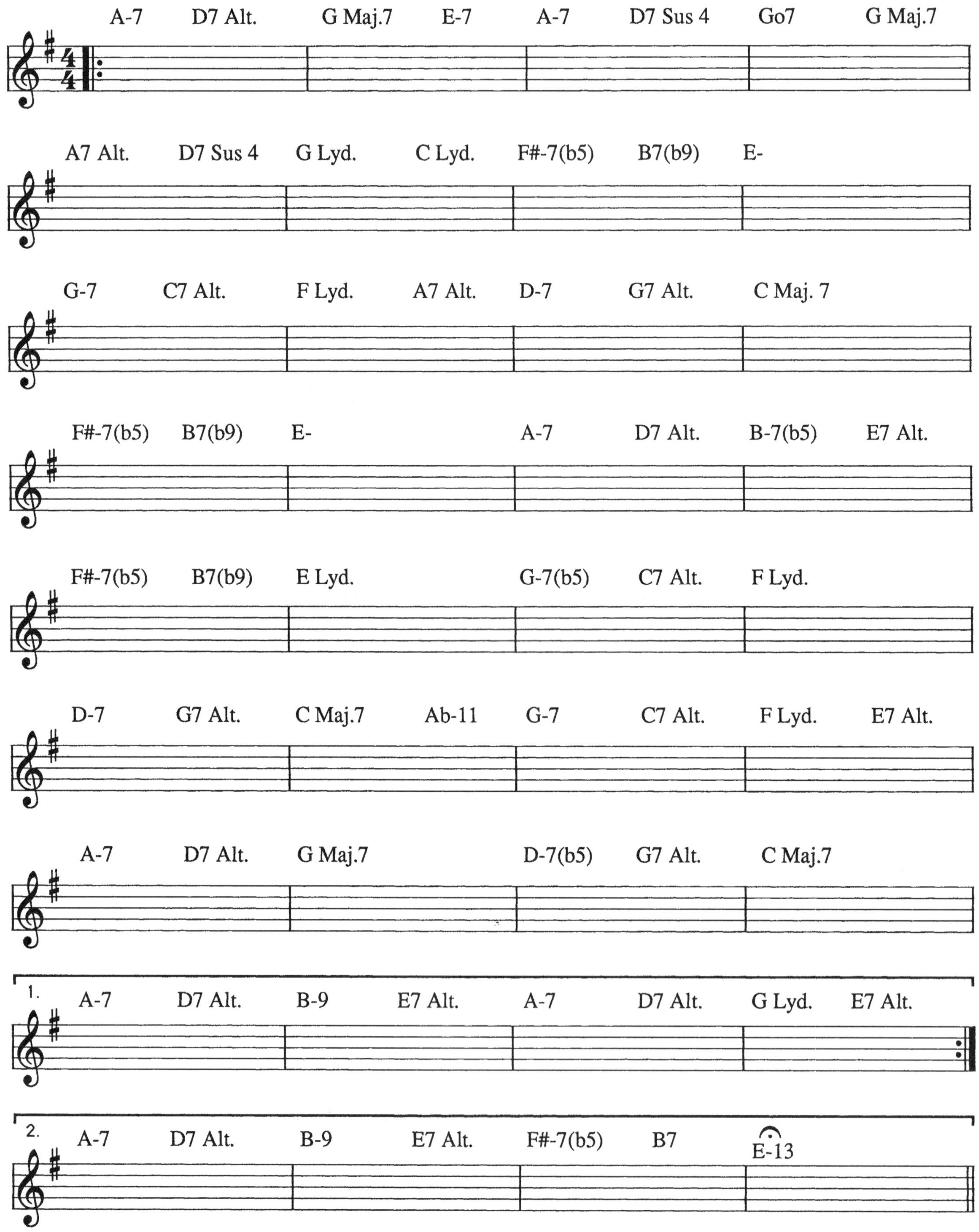
A-7 D7 Alt. G Maj.7 E-7 A-7 D7 Sus 4 Go7 G Maj.7
A7 Alt. D7 Sus 4 G Lyd. C Lyd. F#-7(b5) B7(b9) E-
G-7 C7 Alt. F Lyd. A7 Alt. D-7 G7 Alt. C Maj. 7
F#-7(b5) B7(b9) E- A-7 D7 Alt. B-7(b5) E7 Alt.
F#-7(b5) B7(b9) E Lyd. G-7(b5) C7 Alt. F Lyd.
D-7 G7 Alt. C Maj.7 Ab-11 G-7 C7 Alt. F Lyd. E7 Alt.
A-7 D7 Alt. G Maj.7 D-7(b5) G7 Alt. C Maj.7
1. A-7 D7 Alt. B-9 E7 Alt. A-7 D7 Alt. G Lyd. E7 Alt.
2. A-7 D7 Alt. B-9 E7 Alt. F#-7(b5) B7 E-13

Observations

- I couldn't use the D Dorian voicings because of the "low D" tuning, but I did transpose them up a whole step! (Last two voicings of harmonic continuity).
- In the first page, all C major 7th chords are bracketed, chord symbols are simplified. Analyze and be aware of all chord tones and tensions in all voicings.
- In harmonic continuity, chord symbols are used only on "passing chords" (a little "artistic liberty") that were not included on page 68.
- Notice all C major 7th chords on pages 68 and 69. (Brackets are omitted on page 70). Notice all other major 7th chords on pages 68 and 69. (FM7, GM7, BbM7, DM7).
- It might be a good idea to write a melody for this harmonic continuity. Then, start improvising on the changes.
- Think of all the other tonalities that could have been used if I had been able to transpose the C Major 7th chord!
- The harmonic continuity is a very good study in four, five, and six part voicings. Study voice leading carefully.
- You might have to use a tape recorder to play all the notes in the voicings (or another guitarist; or a bass player).

Uses of C major 7 b5

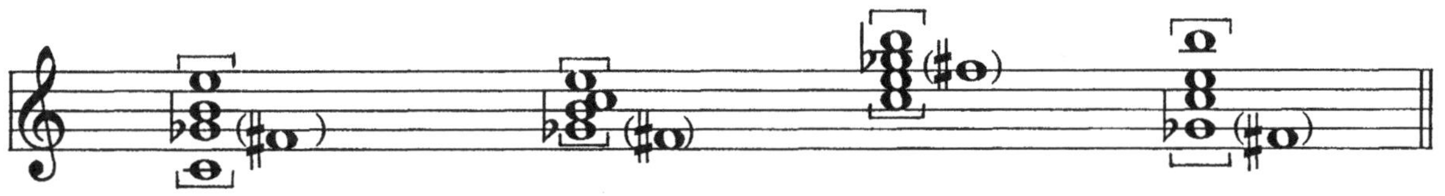

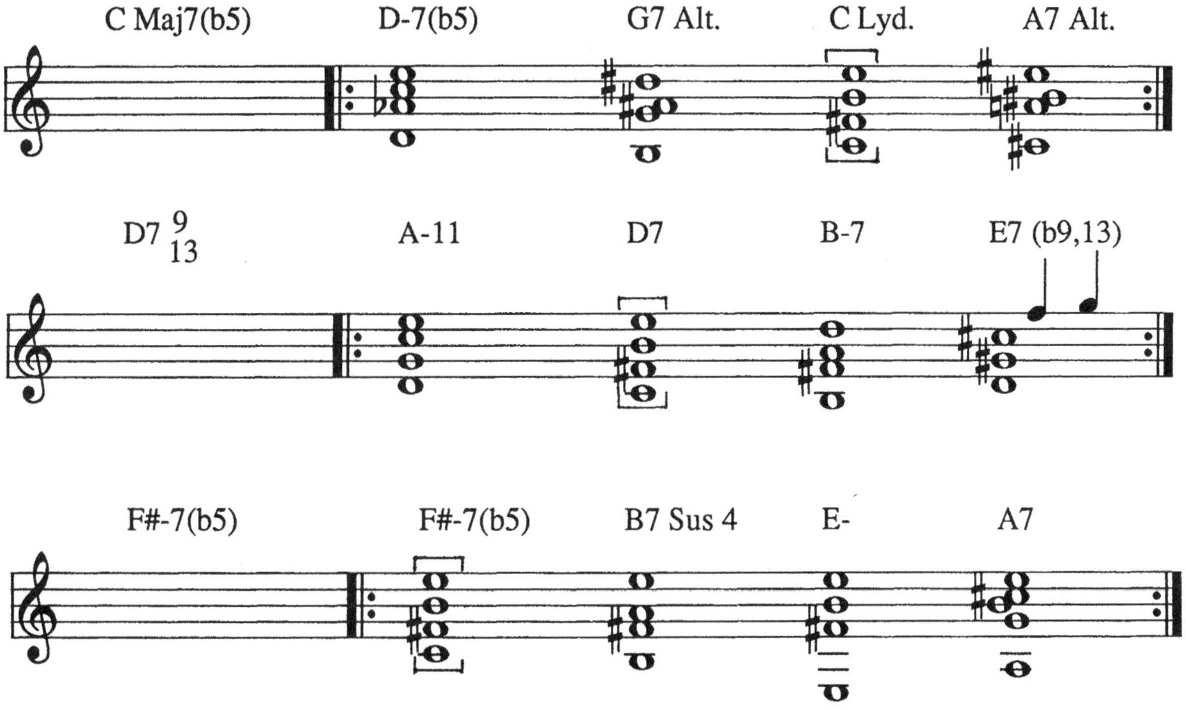
C Maj7(b5)
D-7(b5)
G7 Alt.
C Lyd.
A7 Alt.
D7 9 13
A-11
D7
B-7
E7 (b9,13)
F#-7(b5)
F#-7(b5)
B7 Sus 4
E-
A7

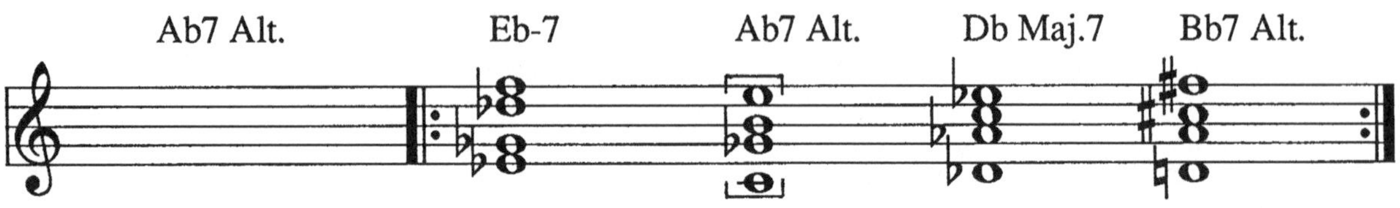
Ab7 Alt.
Eb-7
Ab7 Alt.
Db Maj.7
Bb7 Alt.

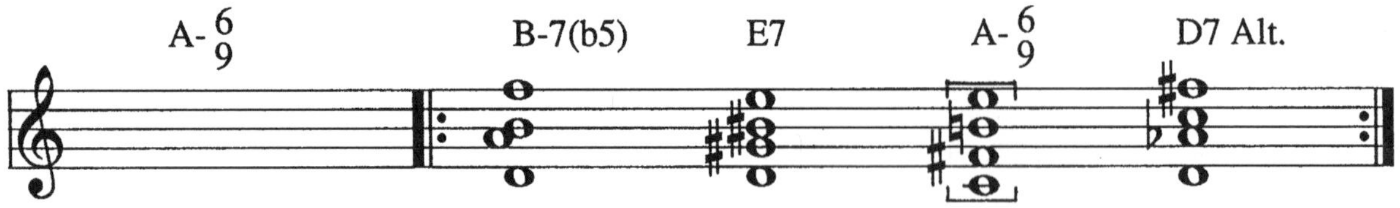
A- 6/9
B-7(b5)
E7
A- 6/9
D7 Alt.

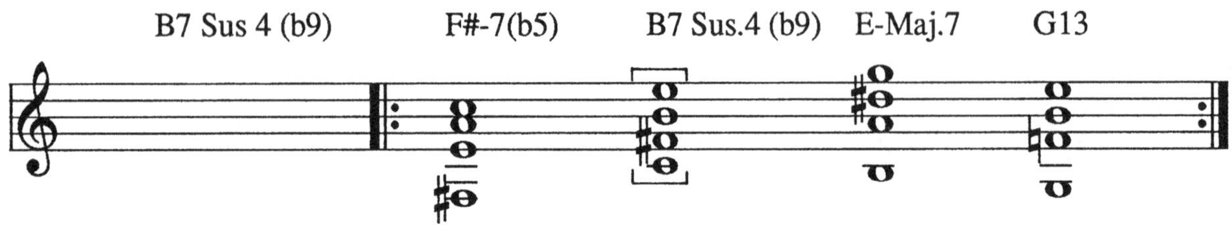
B7 Sus 4 (b9)
F#-7(b5)
B7 Sus.4 (b9)
E-Maj.7
G13

Step 1. Write three or more variations for each of the six uses (three or four per variation). Use the three voicings above for the three variations (or use others, if you prefer).

Step 2. Write a progression using at least 75% of the material you came up with (add passing chords if you like).

Step 3. Write a melody.

Step 4. Write out changes and begin improvising.

Question:
Can you find six different Major (b5) chords in the previous harmonic continuity?

Uses of Aug. Maj. 7 Chord

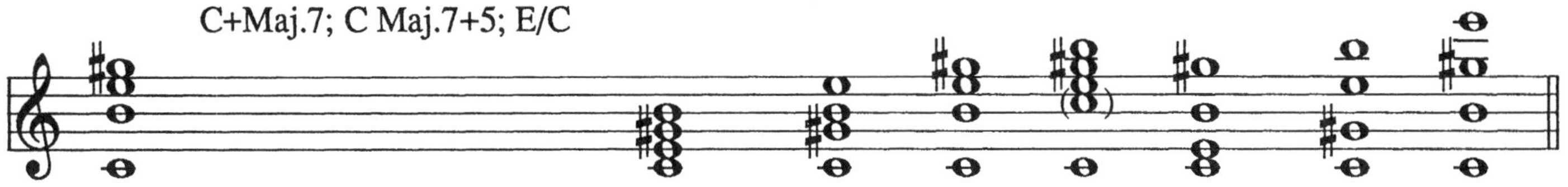
C+Maj.7; C Maj.7+5; E/C

Tonic Substitute

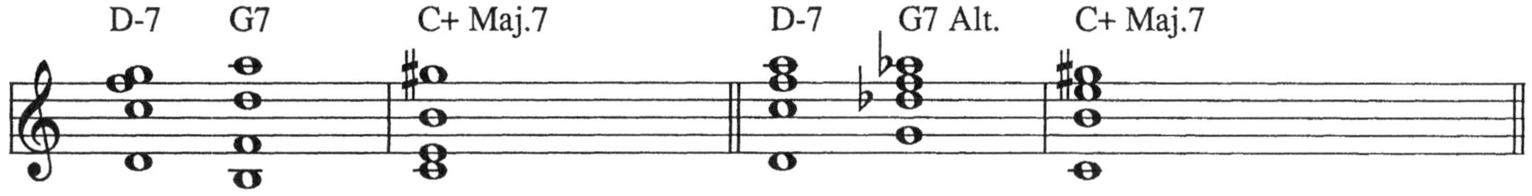
D-7
G7
C+ Maj.7
D-7
G7 Alt.
C+ Maj.7

Dominant Substitute (for C7)

C+Maj.7 is particularly Interesting in that it is a way to harmonize the natural 7 on a Dom.7 chord.

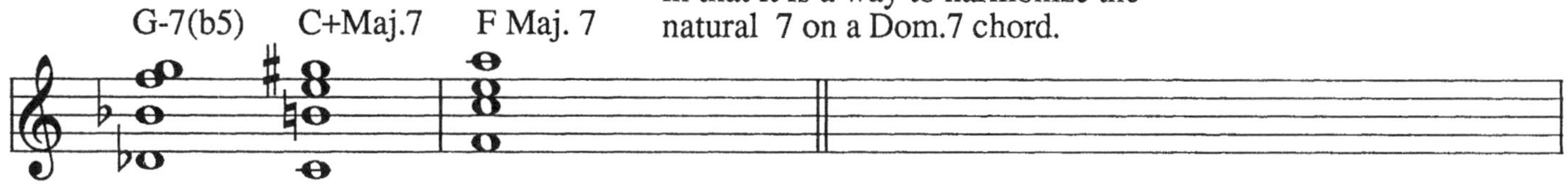
G-7(b5)
C+Maj.7
F Maj. 7

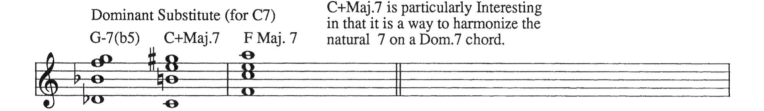

Five uses derived from Melodic Minor modes:

C+M7 is the III chord in A Melodic Minor; consequently we shall see that it can be substituted or used for A- (I); D Lyd. b7 (IV); G#7 alt. (VII); and B7 sus4(b9,13); and that, in fact, all If these chords are somewhat interchangable!!

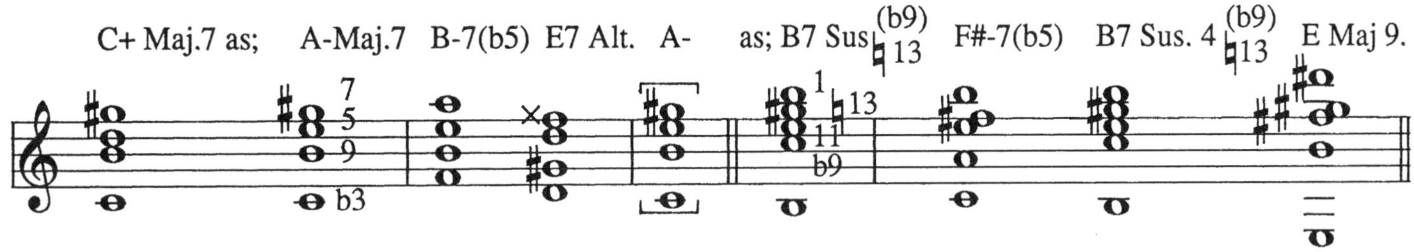
C+ Maj.7 as;
A-Maj.7
B-7(b5)
E7 Alt.
A-
as; B7 Sus (b9) ♮13
F#-7(b5)
B7 Sus. 4 (b9) ♮13
E Maj 9.
7
5
9
b3
1
♮13
11
b9

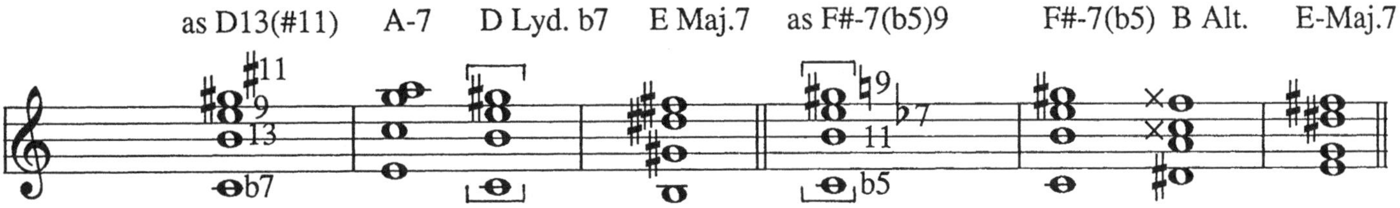
as D13(#11)
A-7
D Lyd. b7
E Maj.7
as F#-7(b5)9
F#-7(b5)
B Alt.
E-Maj.7
#11
9
13
b7
♮9
♭7
11
b5

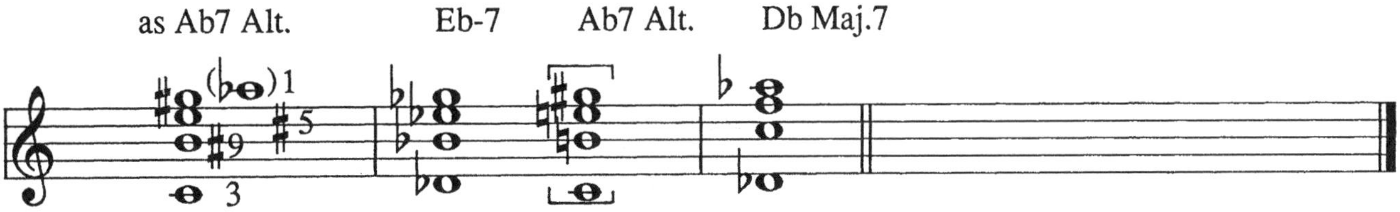
as Ab7 Alt.
Eb-7
Ab7 Alt.
Db Maj.7
1
#9
#5
3

Triads Over Bass Notes: I

There are 48 possible triads over any bass note. Twelve of these 48 turn out to be just a triad with one of the notes doubled in the bass. Therefore, we'll eliminate them. Using C as the bass note, these "redundant" structures would be:

C	C-	C+	C°;	E+;	F	F-	F#° ;	Ab	Ab+ ;	A-	A°
C	C	C	C	C	C	C	C	C	C	C	C

In addition, we have some repetition of structures, since the twelve augmented triads are really only four augmented triads. C+ (E+; Ab+) was already eliminated above because of "redundancy." The remaining nine augmented triads are really only three. We'll write them like this:

Db+ (F+; A+) Bb+ (F#+; D+) B+ (Eb+; G+)

This means that, out of 48 possibilities, only 30 turn out to be structuresof four different notes:

Db	Db-	Db°	D	D-	D°	Eb	Eb-	Eb°	E	E-	E°	F°
C	C	C	C	C	C	C	C	C	C	C	C	C
F#	F#-	G	G-	G°	Ab-	Ab°	A	Bb	Bb-	Bb°	B	B-	B°
C	C	C	C	C	C	C	C	C	C	C	C	C	C

Db+(F+;A+)	Bb+(F#+;D+)	B+(Eb+;G+)
C	C	C

These 30 structures fall into three convenient types:

1. Obvious 7th chords (8)
2. Less obvious 7th chords (7)
3. Hybrid structures (15)

Let's list them:

Obvious 7th chords (8):

Eb/C = C-7; Eb-/C = C-7(b5); Eb°/C = C°7

G+(B+; Eb+)/C = C- M7; E/C = C+ M7; E-/C = CM7

B/C = C tonic diminished

Less obvious 7th chords (7):

Db/C = DbM7; Db-/C = Db-M7; Db°/C = D tonic dim.

D/C = D7; D-/C = D-7(F6); D°/C = D-7(b5) F-6

Db+(F+; A+)/C = Db+M7

Hybrid structures (15):

F°; F# F#-; G G- G°; Ab- Ab°; A;
C C C C C C C C C

Bb Bb- Bb°; B- B° ; Bb+(F#+; D+)
C C C C C C

These hybrid structures can be analyzed as incomplete 9th, 11th, and13th chords.

All 30 possibilities are useful. Not only are all 30 useful, but *each* can be used in at least several ways. (See "six Uses of CMaj. 7"; "Uses of C+M7).")

In order to explore this material thoroughly, you'll have to take *each* of the 30 structures and analyze it in all 12 keys.

Example: D/C = C° 7, Cly., Clydb7, D7, Eb° 7, E-7 (b5, 9), F7, F#7 alt., F#° 7; Ab7 alt., A-6(11); Bb+M7(9); B7(#9,b9)

Even though you could come up with all the possible uses on paper, don't expect that you'll be able to use them all in context right away. That could take some time. You'll find that you may not really like the sound of some of them. If that's the case, then don't use them. Out of all the material that you generate, you'll be doing well if you can actually incorporate 10% into your playing. But having all the possibilities known is very useful because you can always come back to the unexplored material later on.

Observations

- Each of the 30 possibilities has many inversions on the guitar.
- Don't forget that you could try to voice these chords with the triad spread position as well as closed:

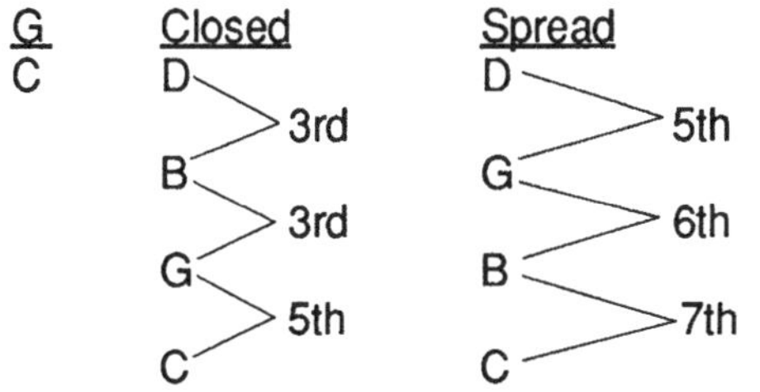
G
C
Closed
D
3rd
B
3rd
G
5th
C
Spread
D
5th
G
6th
B
7th
C

- You'll have a hard time finding all of these chords if you don't know your triads fairly well.
- It's also very possible to arrive at other structures by putting the bass note above the triad or in the middle somewhere. (In other words, the "bass note" does not always have to be the lowest note of the voicing).

F#
C

- All 30 structures could be arpeggiated in countless ways. If you take the four different notes of a particular structure and compress them into one octave, you'll have many different four-note scales for interesting melodic possibilities.

- Three-part 4th voicings could also work over bass notes!

Triads Over Bass Notes: II

The next few pages include some examples of a different way to use triads over bass notes. We aren't concerned with figuring out all the possible uses for each chord. We take a particular structure and move it through either three-or four-note tonic systems. (A three-note tonic system would be an augmented triad; a 4 note system would be a diminished 7th chord.) Be sure to voice-lead the upper structures very carefully. These progressions have an interesting effect which is the result of the fact that, although each structure is the same chord type, the symmetrical bass motion (in conjunction with the non-parallel triadic voice-leading) "disguises" the sameness of sound that might occur otherwise.

Keep in mind that (as was mentioned before) you could spread the triad and you could put the bass note anywhere else in the voicing that you wanted.

G-	Bb-	C#-	E-	Bb-	C#-	E-	G-	C#-	E-	G-	Bb-	E-	G-	Bb-	C#-
E	G	Bb	C#	G	Bb	C#	E	Bb	C#	E	G	C#	E	G	Bb
Ab-	B-	D-	F-	B-	D-	F-	Ab-	D-	F-	Ab-	B-	F-	Ab-	B-	D-
F	Ab	B	D	Ab	B	D	F	B	D	F	Ab	D	F	Ab	B
A-	C-	Eb-	F#-	C-	Eb-	F#-	A-	Eb-	F#-	A-	C-	F#-	A-	C-	Eb-
F#	A	C	Eb	A	C	Eb	F#	C	Eb	F#	A	Eb	F#	A	C
E-	C#-	Bb-	G-	G-	E-	C#-	Bb-	Bb-	G-	E-	C#-	C#-	Bb-	G-	E-
C#	Bb	G	E	E	C#	Bb	G	G	E	C#	Bb	Bb	G	E	C#

F-	D-	B-	Ab-	Ab	F-	D-	B-	B-	Ab-	F-	D-	D-	B-	Ab-	F-
D	B	Ab	F	F	D	B	Ab	Ab	F	D	B	B	Ab	F	D

F#-	Eb-	C-	A-	A-	F#-	Eb-	C-	C-	A-	F#-	Eb-	Eb-	C-	A-	F#-
Eb	C	A	F#	F#	Eb	C	A	A	F#	Eb	C	C	A	F#	Eb

G-	Bb-	C#-	E-	Bb-	C#-	E-	G-	C#-	E-	G-	Bb-	E-	G-	Bb-	C#-
C#	E	G	Bb	E	G	Bb	C#	G	Bb	C#	E	Bb	C#	E	G

Ab-	B-	D-	F-	B-	D-	F-	Ab-	D-	F-	Ab-	B-	F-	Ab-	B-	D-
D	F	Ab	B	F	Ab	B	D	Ab	B	D	F	B	D	F	Ab

A-	C-	Eb-	F#-	C-	Eb-	F#-	A-	Eb-	F#-	A-	C-	F#-	A-	C-	Eb-
Eb	F#	A	C	F#	A	C	Eb	A	C	Eb	F#	C	Eb	F#	A

E-	C#-	Bb-	G-	G-	E-	C#-	Bb-	Bb-	G-	E-	C#-	C#-	Bb-	G-	E-
Bb	G	E	C#	C#	Bb	G	E	E	C#	Bb	G	G	E	C#	Bb

F-	D-	B-	Ab-	Ab-	F-	D-	B-	B-	Ab-	F-	D-	D-	B-	Ab-	F-
B	Ab	F	D	D	B	Ab	F	F	D	B	Ab	Ab	F	D	B

F#-	Eb-	C-	A-	A-	F#-	Eb-	C-	C-	A-	F#-	Eb-	Eb-	C-	A-	F#-
C	A	F#	Eb	Eb	C	A	F#	F#	Eb	C	A	A	F#	Eb	C

G-	B-	Eb-	B-	Eb-	G-	Eb-	G-	B-	Eb-	B-	G-	B-	G-	Eb-	G-	Eb-	B-
E	Ab	C	Ab	C	E	C	E	Ab	C	Ab	E	Ab	E	C	E	C	Ab

Ab-	C-	E-	C-	E-	Ab-	E-	Ab-	C-	E-	C-	Ab-	C-	Ab-	E-	Ab-	E-	C-
F	A	C#	A	C#	F	C#	F	A	C#	A	F	A	F	C#	F	C#	A

A-	Db-	F-	Db-	F-	A-	F-	A-	Db-	F-	Db-	A-	Db-	A-	F-	A-	F-	Db-
F#	Bb	D	Bb	D	F#	D	F#	Bb	D	Bb	F#	Bb	F#	D	F#	D	Bb

G-	B-	Eb-	B-	Eb-	G-	Eb-	G-	B-	Eb-	B-	G-	B-	G-	Eb-	G-	Eb-	B-
Ab	C	E	C	E	Ab	E	Ab	C	E	C	Ab	C	Ab	E	Ab	E	C

G#-	C-	E-	C-	E-	G#-	E-	G#-	C-	E-	C-	G#-	C-	G#-	E-	G#-	E-	C-
A	Db	F	Db	F	A	F	A	Db	F	Db	A	Db	A	F	A	F	Db

A-	C#-	F-	C#-	F-	A-	F-	A-	C#-	F-	C#-	A-	C#-	A-	F-	A-	F-	C#-
Bb	D	Gb	D	Gb	Bb	Gb	Bb	D	Gb	D	Bb	D	Bb	Gb	Bb	Gb	D

A#-	D-	F#-	D-	F#-	A#-	F#-	A#-	D-	F#-	D-	A#-	D-	A#-	F#-	A#-	F#-	D-
B	Eb	G	Eb	G	B	G	B	Eb	G	Eb	B	Eb	B	G	B	G	Eb

G-	B-	Eb-	B-	Eb-	G-	Eb-	G-	B-	Eb-	B-	G-	B-	G-	Eb-	G-	Eb-	B-
C	E	Ab	E	Ab	C	Ab	C	E	Ab	E	C	E	C	Ab	C	Ab	E

Ab-	C-	E-	C-	E-	Ab-	E-	Ab-	C-	E-	C-	Ab-	C-	Ab-	E-	Ab-	E-	C-
Db	F	A	F	A	Db	A	Db	F	A	F	Db	F	Db	A	Db	A	F

A-	Db-	F-	Db-	F-	A-	F-	A-	Db-	F-	Db-	A-	Db-	A-	F-	A-	F-	Db-
D	Gb	Bb	Gb	Bb	D	Bb	D	Gb	Bb	Gb	D	Gb	D	Bb	D	Bb	Gb

Bb-	D-	F#-	D-	F#-	Bb-	F#-	Bb-	D-	F#-	D-	Bb-	D-	Bb-	F#-	Bb-	F#-	D-
Eb	G	B	G	B	Eb	B	Eb	G	B	G	Eb	G	Eb	B	Eb	B	G

G-	Bb-	C#-	E-	Bb-	C#-	E-	G-	C#-	E-	G-	Bb-	E-	G-	Bb-	C#-
Eb	Gb	A	C	Gb	A	C	Eb	A	C	Eb	Gb	C	Eb	Gb	A

G#-	B-	D-	F-	B-	D-	F-	G#-	D-	F-	G#-	B-	F-	G#-	B-	D-
E	G	Bb	Db	G	Bb	Db	E	Bb	Db	E	G	Db	E	G	Bb

A-	C-	Eb-	F#-	C-	Eb-	F#-	A-	Eb-	F#-	A-	C-	F#-	A-	C-	Eb-
F	Ab	B	D	Ab	B	D	F	B	D	F	Ab	D	F	Ab	B

G-	Bb-	C#-	E-	Bb-	C#-	E-	G-	C#-	E-	G-	Bb-	E-	G-	Bb-	C#-
F#	A	C	Eb	A	C	Eb	F#	C	Eb	F#	A	Eb	F#	A	C
G#-	B-	D-	F-	B-	D-	F-	G#-	D-	F-	G#-	B-	F-	G#-	B-	D-
G	Bb	C#	E	Bb	C#	E	G	C#	E	G	Bb	E	G	Bb	C#
A-	C-	Eb-	F#-	C-	Eb-	F#-	A-	Eb-	F#-	A-	C-	F#-	A-	C-	Eb-
Ab	B	D	F	B	D	F	Ab	D	F	Ab	B	F	Ab	B	D
G-	Bb-	Db-	E-	Bb-	Db-	E-	G-	Db-	E-	G-	Bb-	E-	G-	Bb-	Db-
A	C	Eb	F#	C	Eb	F#	A	Eb	F#	A	C	F#	A	C	Eb
Ab-	B-	D-	F-	B-	D-	F-	Ab-	D-	F-	Ab-	B-	F-	Ab-	B-	D-
Bb	Db	E	G	Db	E	G	Bb	E	G	Bb	Db	G	Bb	Db	E-
A-	C-	Eb-	F#-	C-	Eb-	F#-	A-	Eb-	F#-	A-	C-	F#-	A-	C-	Eb-
B	D	F	Ab	D	F	Ab	B	F	Ab	B	D	Ab	B	D	F
G-	Bb-	Db-	E-	Bb-	Db-	E-	G-	Db-	E-	G-	Bb-	E-	G-	Bb-	Db-
C	Eb	Gb	A	Eb	Gb	A	C	Gb	A	C	Eb	A	C	Eb	Gb
Ab-	B-	D-	F-	B-	D-	F-	Ab-	D-	F-	Ab-	B-	F-	Ab-	B-	D-
Db	E	G	Bb	E	G	Bb	Db	G	Bb	Db	E	Bb	Db	E	G
A-	C-	Eb-	Gb-	C-	Eb-	Gb-	A-	Eb-	Gb-	A-	C-	Gb-	A-	C-	Eb-
D	F	Ab	B	F	Ab	B	D	Ab	B	D	F	B	D	F	Ab
D	F	Ab	B	F	Ab	B	D	Ab	B	D	F	B	D	F	Ab
E	G	Bb	Db	G	Bb	Db	E	Bb	Db	E	G	Db	E	G	Bb
Eb	F#	A	C	F#	A	C	Eb	A	C	Eb	F#	C	Eb	F#	A
F	Ab	B	D	Ab	B	D	F	B	D	F	Ab	D	F	Ab	B
E	G	Bb	Db	G	Bb	Db	E	Bb	Db	E	G	Db	E	G	Bb
F#	A	C	Eb	A	C	Eb	F#	C	Eb	F#	A	Eb	F#	A	C
D	F	Ab	B	F	Ab	B	D	Ab	B	D	F	B	D	F	Ab
G	Bb	Db	E	Bb	Db	E	G	Db	E	G	Bb	E	G	Bb	Db
Eb	F#	A	C	F#	A	C	Eb	A	C	Eb	F#	C	Eb	F#	A
Ab	B	D	F	B	D	F	Ab	D	F	Ab	B	F	Ab	B	D
E	G	Bb	Db	G	Bb	Db	E	Bb	Db	E	G	Db	E	G	Bb
A	C	Eb	Gb	C	Eb	Gb	A	Eb	Gb	A	C	Gb	A	C	Eb
D	F	Ab	B	F	Ab	B	D	Ab	B	D	F	B	D	F	Ab
Bb	Db	E	G	Db	E	G	Bb	E	G	Bb	Db	G	Bb	Db	E
Eb	F#	A	C	F#	A	C	Eb	A	C	Eb	F#	C	Eb	F#	A
B	D	F	Ab	D	F	Ab	B	F	Ab	B	D	Ab	B	D	F
E	G	Bb	Db	G	Bb	Db	E	Bb	Db	E	G	Db	E	G	Bb
C	Eb	Gb	A	Eb	Gb	A	C	Gb	A	C	Eb	A	C	Eb	Gb
D	F	Ab	B	F	Ab	B	D	Ab	B	D	F	B	D	F	Ab
Db	E	G	Bb	E	G	Bb	Db	G	Bb	Db	E	Bb	Db	E	G
Eb	Gb	A	C	Gb	A	C	Eb	A	C	Eb	Gb	C	Eb	Gb	A
D	F	Ab	B	F	Ab	B	D	Ab	B	D	F	B	D	F	Ab
E	G	Bb	Db	G	Bb	Db	E	Bb	Db	E	G	Db	E	G	Bb
Eb	Gb	A	C	Gb	A	C	Eb	A	C	Eb	Gb	C	Eb	Gb	A

4th Voicings

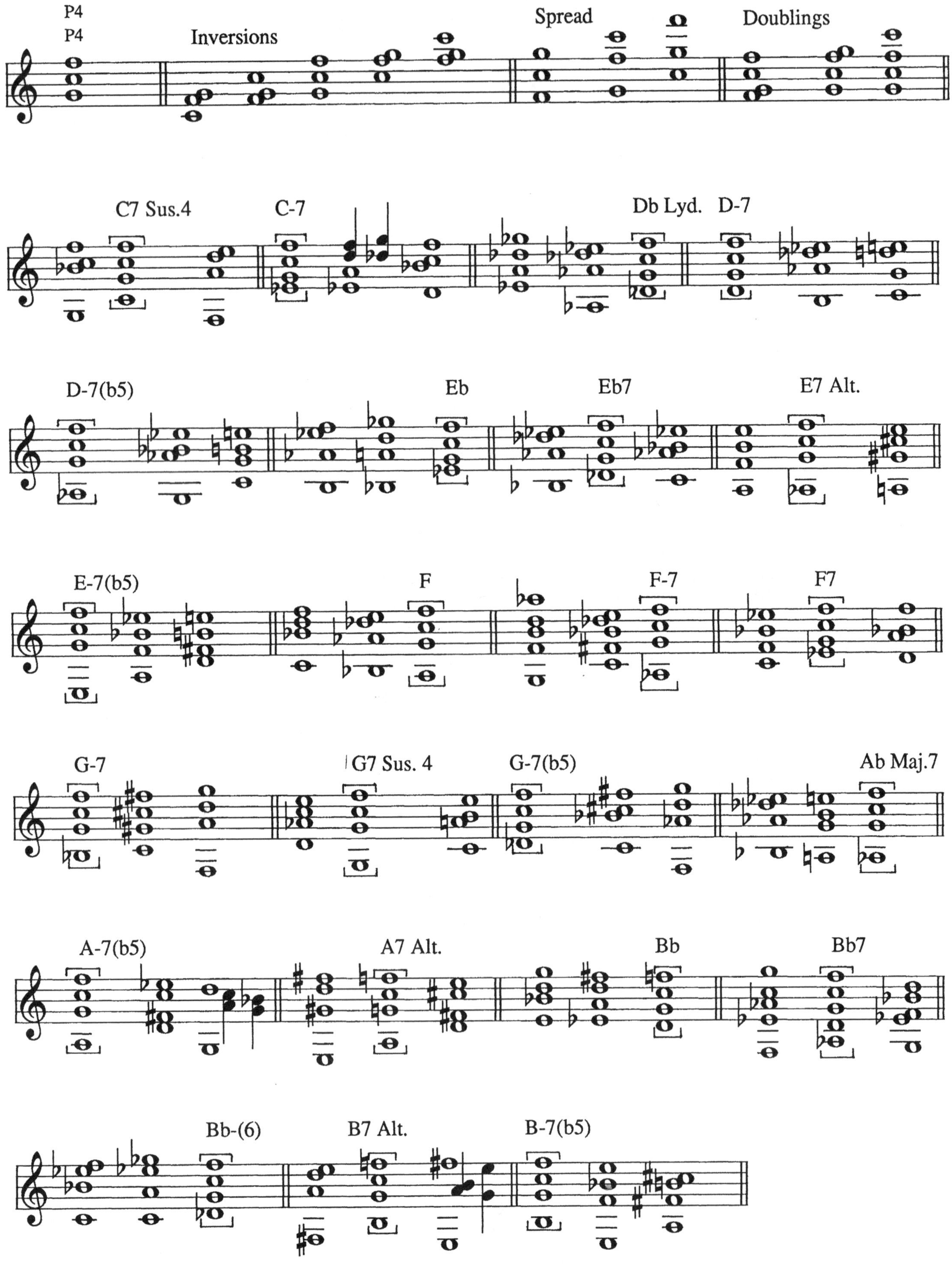
P4
P4
Inversions
Spread
Doublings
C7 Sus.4
C-7
Db Lyd.
D-7
D-7(b5)
Eb
Eb7
E7 Alt.
E-7(b5)
F
F-7
F7
G-7
G7 Sus. 4
G-7(b5)
Ab Maj.7
A-7(b5)
A7 Alt.
Bb
Bb7
Bb-(6)
B7 Alt.
B-7(b5)

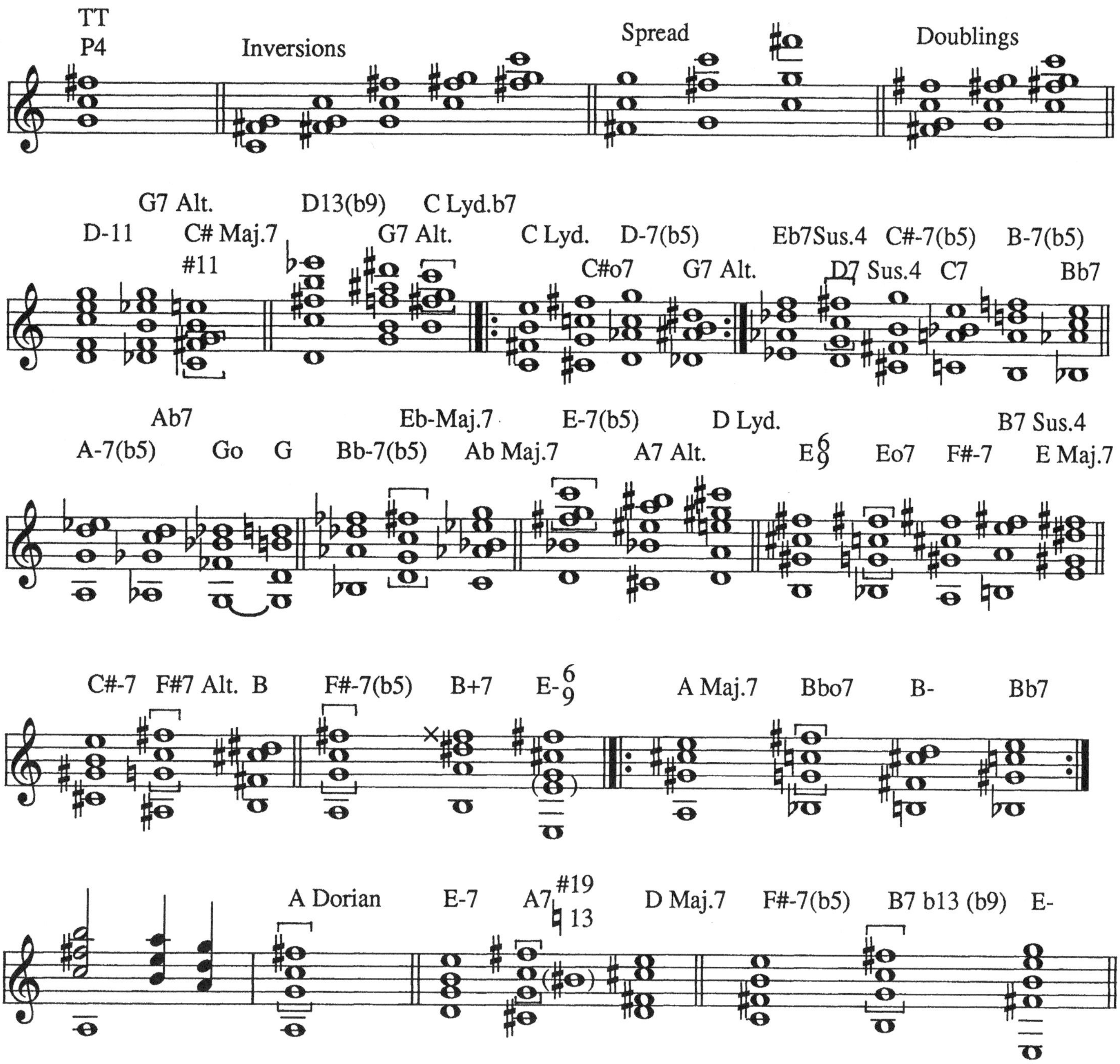
TT
P4
Inversions
Spread
Doublings
G7 Alt.
D-11
C# Maj.7
#11
D13(b9)
G7 Alt.
C Lyd.b7
C Lyd.
D-7(b5)
C#o7
G7 Alt.
Eb7Sus.4
D7 Sus.4
C#-7(b5)
C7
B-7(b5)
Bb7
Ab7
A-7(b5)
Go
G
Bb-7(b5)
Eb-Maj.7
Ab Maj.7
E-7(b5)
A7 Alt.
D Lyd.
E 6/9
Eo7
F#-7
B7 Sus.4
E Maj.7
C#-7
F#7 Alt.
B
F#-7(b5)
B+7
E- 6/9
A Maj.7
Bbo7
B-
Bb7
A Dorian
E-7
A7 #19 ♮13
D Maj.7
F#-7(b5)
B7 b13 (b9)
E-

Fill in the missings voicings.

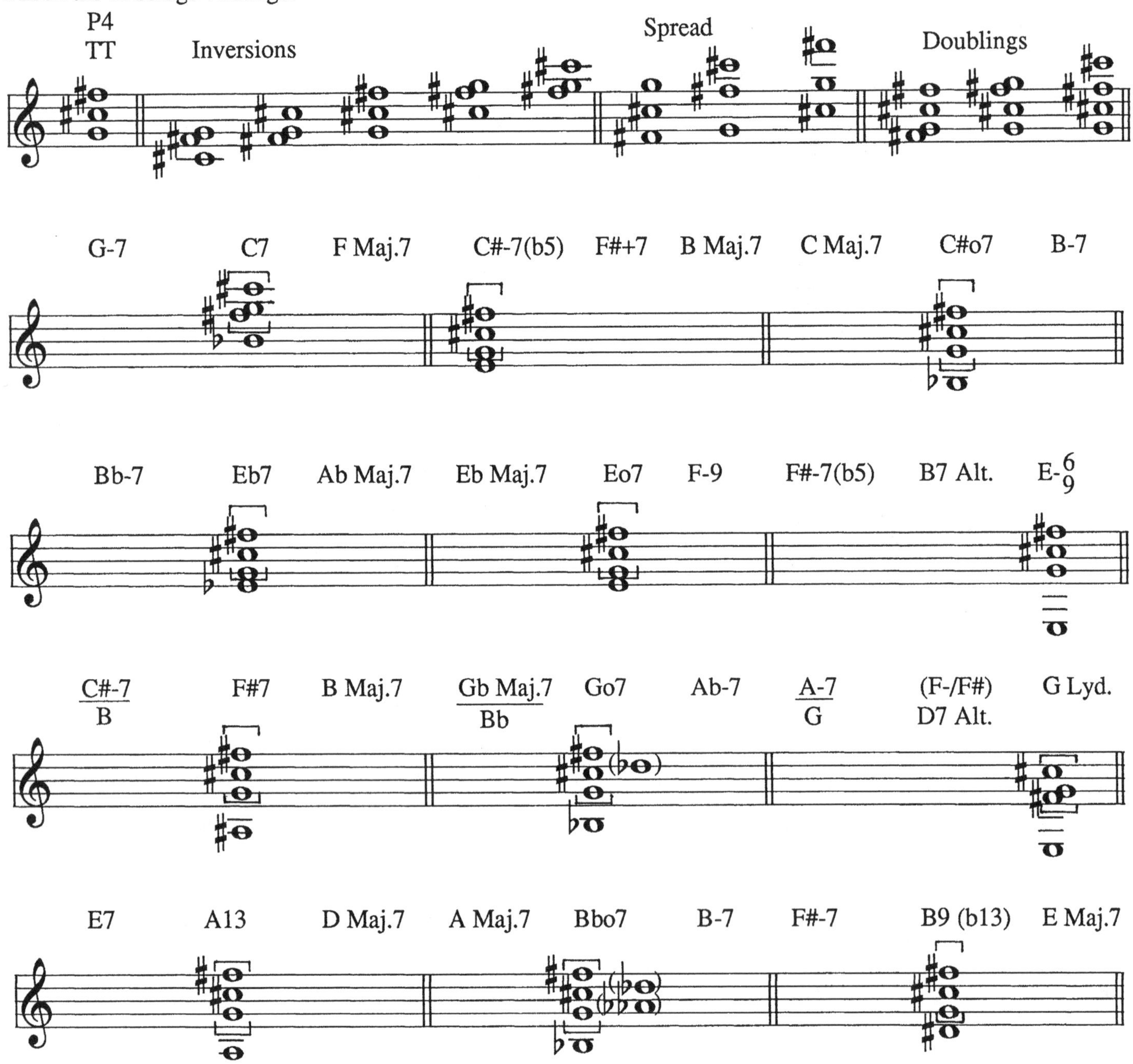

P4
TT
Inversions
Spread
Doublings
G-7
C7
F Maj.7
C#-7(b5)
F#+7
B Maj.7
C Maj.7
C#o7
B-7
Bb-7
Eb7
Ab Maj.7
Eb Maj.7
Eo7
F-9
F#-7(b5)
B7 Alt.
E-6/9
C#-7/B
F#7
B Maj.7
Gb Maj.7/Bb
Go7
Ab-7
A-7/G
(F-/F#)
D7 Alt.
G Lyd.
E7
A13
D Maj.7
A Maj.7
Bbo7
B-7
F#-7
B9 (b13)
E Maj.7

Three-Part 4th Voicings Over Bass Notes

36 -9 = 27: four-part structures (The 9 structures in parentheses are redundant as they contain two C's.)

B	Bb	B	B	B#	B#	C	C#	C#	Db	D	D	D	D#	D#	Eb	E	E
F	F	F#	F#	F#	F##	G	G	G	Ab	Ab	A	A	A	A#	Bb	Bb	B
C	C	C	C#	C#	C#	D	D	D	Eb	Eb	Eb	E	E	E	F	F	F
C	C	C	C	C	C	C	C	C	C	C	C	C	C	C	C	C	C

E	E#	E#	F	F#	F#	Gb	G	G	G	G#	G#	Ab	A	A	A	A#	A#
B	B	B#	C	C	C#	Db	Db	D	D	D	D#	Eb	Eb	E	E	E	E#
F#	F#	F#	G	G	G	Ab	Ab	Ab	A	A	A	Bb	Bb	Bb	B	B	B
C	C	C	C	C	C	C	C	C	C	C	C	C	C	C	C	C	C

22 useful structures:
Match the descriptions below to the appropriate voicings above.

1. Ab/Db
2. C6,9 (from major pentatonic scale)
3. V chord from F. harm. min.
4. Ab13#9 (dim. scale)
5. A°/Bb
6. C7 with 3 *and* sus 4
7. A-/D
8. A-M7(11); D7#11 F#-7(b5,9); Ab alt.
9. C7#9 (from dim. scale/ also alt. dom.)
10. A° or C-6,9/D
11. Ab/Bb
12. G13/C ; F lyd.; D dorian
13. Four-part perfect 4th voicing
14. A-/Bb
15. C7 alt.
16. A-/B
17. Ab lyd.; C aeolian; E7alt; F-6,9
18. CM7b5
19. Ab/D
20. A°/E
21. C7(b9 #11) (symmetrical dim. scale)
22. Ab/A

5 "Weird" Structures:

B	C#	C#	A#	A#
F#	G	G#	E	E#
C#	D	D	B	B
C	C	C	C	C

Pentatonic Scales

"Penta" means five. Therefore, any five-note scale could be called pentatonic. However, two important five note scales emerge as being very useful:

C	D	E	G	A	Major Pentatonic Scale (Chinese)
1	2	3	5	6	
C	D	Eb	G	A	Minor Pentatonic Scale (Japanese)
1	2	b3	5	6	

Notice that these scales correspond to the major scale and the melodic minor scale with the 4th and 7th degrees omitted. The major pentatonic scale works in all the places a major scale could work. The minor pentatonic scale works in all the places a melodic minor scale could work. In addition, since the C major pentatonic scale is contained in the G melodic minor scale, it would work for some melodic minor modes. Also, since the C minor pentatonic scale is contained in the Bb major scale, it would work for some major modes. Isn't this interesting? (C major pentatonic is also contained in F major scale.)

Dispositionally on the guitar, the major pentatonic scale "falls happily." (After all, the tuning of the guitar is an expanded G major pentatonic scale.) The minor pentatonic is more difficult or a bit less accessible. But work with it, since it's so useful.

Another approach that you might keep in mind is the following: since the "problem areas" in the minor pentatonic scale are the minor 3rd interval between 6 and 1, and especially the major 3rd interval between b3 and 5, sometimes it's advisable to add the 4th degree to get a six-note scale. This "falls more happily" on the guitar and is just about as useful as the five note scale. Another useful five-note scale is:

C D E G Bb

1 2 3 5 b7

It covers some of the modes of the F major scale as well as some of the modes of G melodic minor.

C D E G A : C6,9 D-7 **D7 sus4** **E-7(b5)** **FM7** G7sus4 G-7(Dorian only)

(From C major scale
and F major scale) : **A-7** **BbM7#11**

(The chords in **bold** indicate important uses.)

From G melodic min. : G-6 **A7sus4(b9)** C7 **F#7alt.** Bb Lyd.

C D Eb G A : C-6 **D7sus4(b9)** F7 **A-7(b5)** **B7alt.**
(From C mel. min.)

From Bb maj. scale : **EbM7#11** **A-7(b5)** C-7(Dorian only)

C D E G Bb : C7 E-7(b5) **F#7alt.** G-7(dorian only) G-6
A7sus(b9) BbM7#11(weak)

P.S. I almost forgot to mention something very obvious and very important: C major pentatonic works real well for Blues in A! (How many of us started with this?!)

Suggestions

- Check out fingerings for C major pentatonic scale in Positions one through twelve. (Also, Open Position.) Explore Position six a lot. It's absolutely fascinating (and not very easy, at first)! Easy positions are two, five, seven and twelve.

- Check out fingerings for C minor pentatonic scale in Positions Open through twelve. Especially, Positions two, five, seven, ten, and twelve. (Hint: think "2 notes per string)."

- Fingerings for C D E G Bb Penatonic Scale: think "two notes per string."
  1 2 3 5 b7

Major Pentatonic Scale (Scales are shown under staff.)

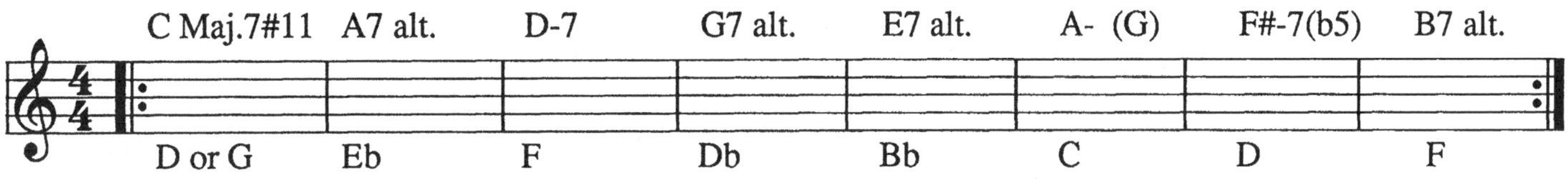
C Maj.7#11
A7 alt.
D-7
G7 alt.
E7 alt.
A- (G)
F#-7(b5)
B7 alt.
D or G
Eb
F
Db
Bb
C
D
F

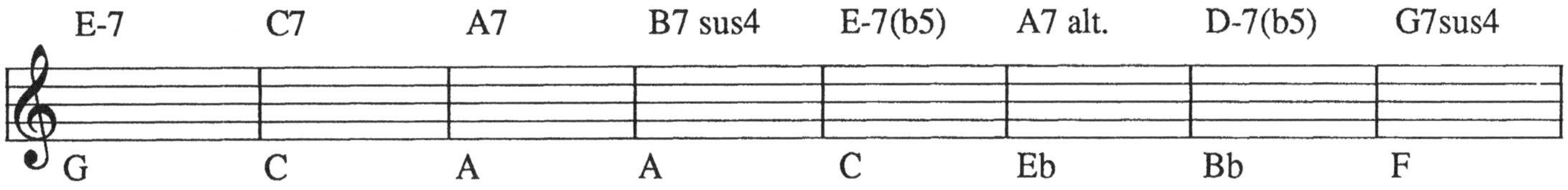
E-7
C7
A7
B7 sus4
E-7(b5)
A7 alt.
D-7(b5)
G7sus4
G
C
A
A
C
Eb
Bb
F

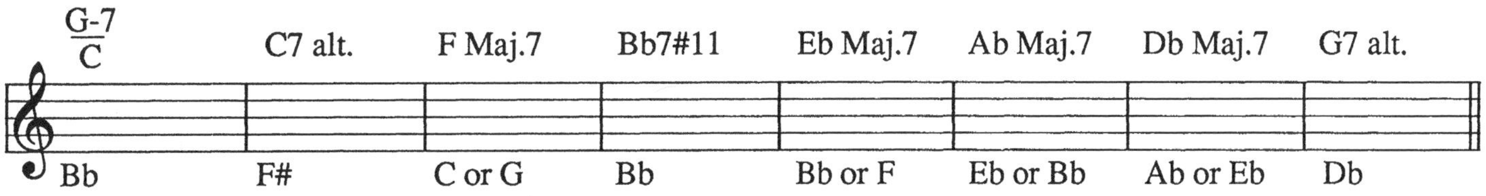
G-7/C
C7 alt.
F Maj.7
Bb7#11
Eb Maj.7
Ab Maj.7
Db Maj.7
G7 alt.
Bb
F#
C or G
Bb
Bb or F
Eb or Bb
Ab or Eb
Db

Minor Pentatonic Scale (Scales are shown under staff.)

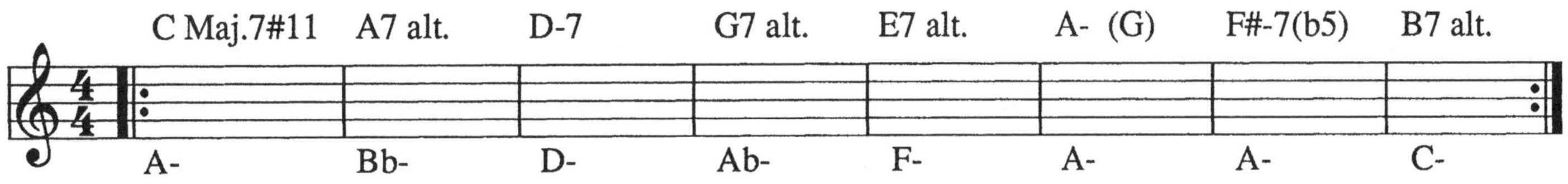
C Maj.7#11
A7 alt.
D-7
G7 alt.
E7 alt.
A- (G)
F#-7(b5)
B7 alt.
A-
Bb-
D-
Ab-
F-
A-
A-
C-

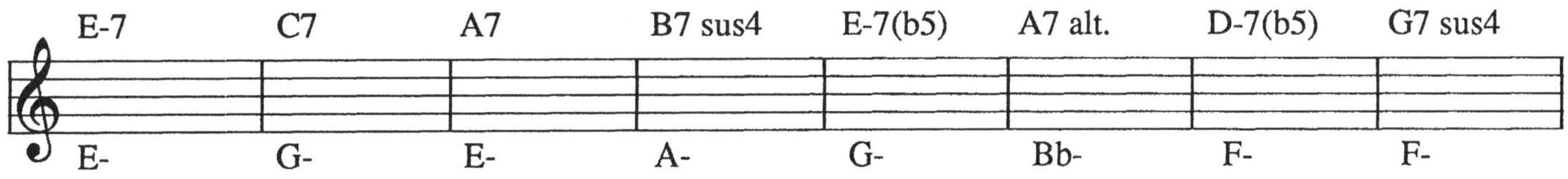
E-7
C7
A7
B7 sus4
E-7(b5)
A7 alt.
D-7(b5)
G7 sus4
E-
G-
E-
A-
G-
Bb-
F-
F-

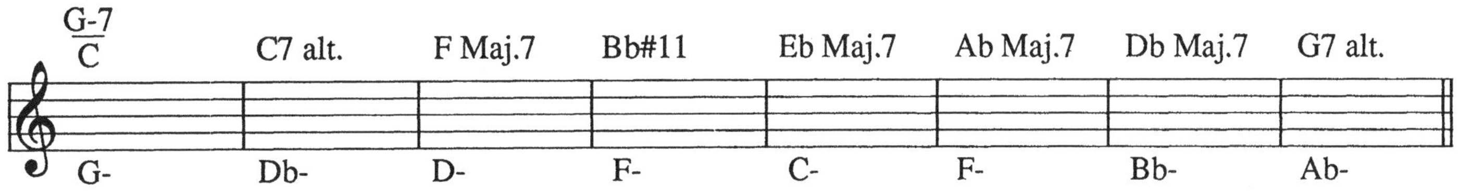
G-7/C
C7 alt.
F Maj.7
Bb#11
Eb Maj.7
Ab Maj.7
Db Maj.7
G7 alt.
G-
Db-
D-
F-
C-
F-
Bb-
Ab-

C Major Pentatonic

Ex. 1 6th Position

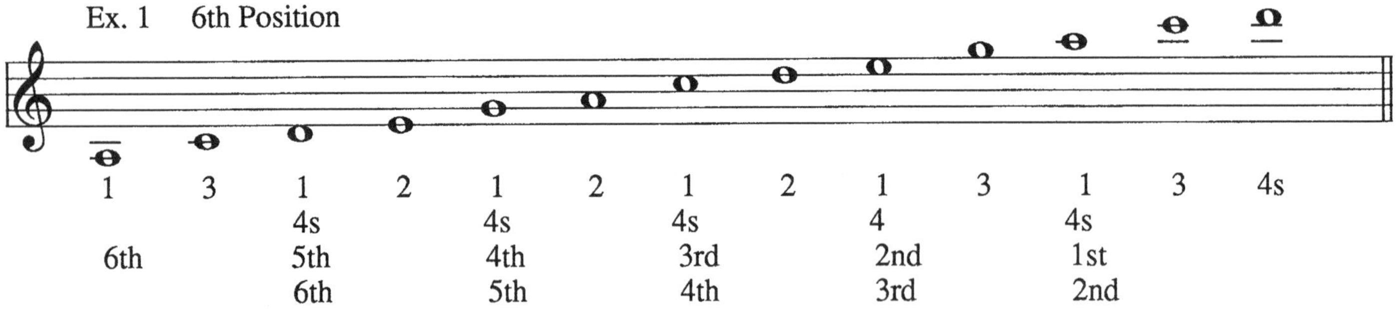
1 3 1 2 1 2 1 2 1 3 1 3 4s
4s 4s 4s 4 4s
6th 5th 4th 3rd 2nd 1st
6th 5th 4th 3rd 2nd

Ex. 2 5th Position

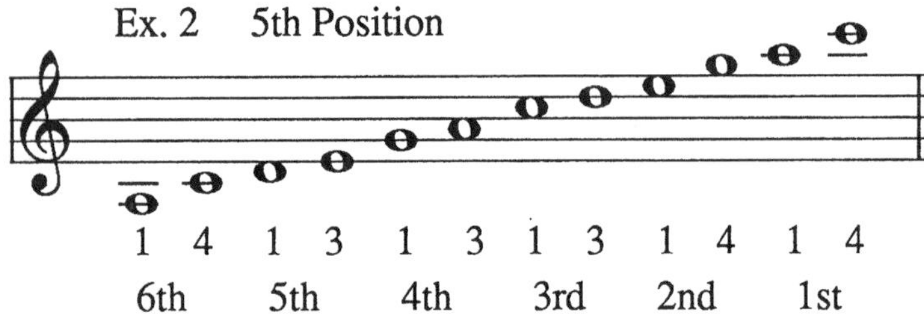
1 4 1 3 1 3 1 3 1 4 1 4
6th 5th 4th 3rd 2nd 1st

Ex. 3 7th Position

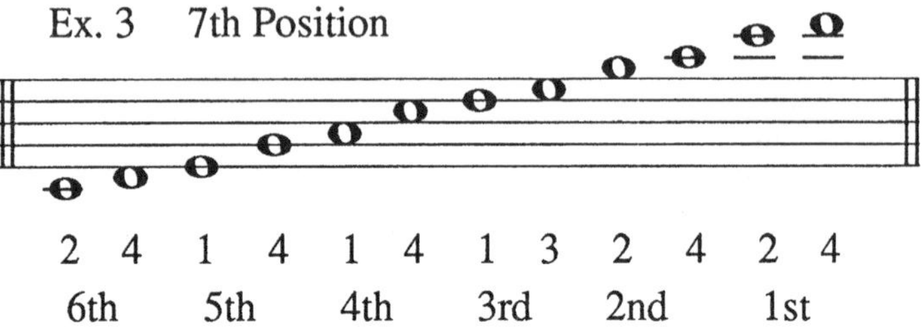
2 4 1 4 1 4 1 3 2 4 2 4
6th 5th 4th 3rd 2nd 1st

Ex. 4 6th Position

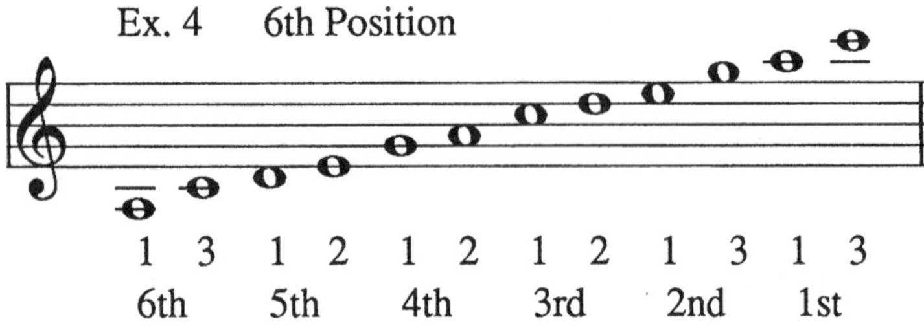
1 3 1 2 1 2 1 2 1 3 1 3
6th 5th 4th 3rd 2nd 1st

Ex. 5 6th Position

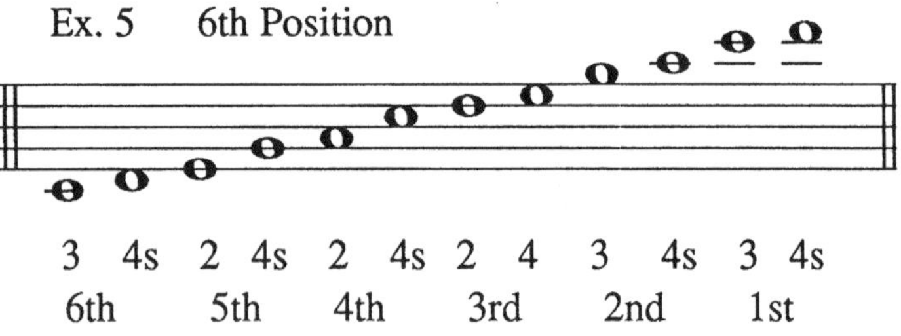
3 4s 2 4s 2 4s 2 4 3 4s 3 4s
6th 5th 4th 3rd 2nd 1st

Observations:

- #4 closely resembles #2 (everyone knows this one!) and is physically and dispositionally just about as easy.
- #5 closely resembles #3 (almost everyone knows this one!) but is physically and dispositionally more difficult. Consequently, #1[sixth position] (which includes both #4 and #5) contains the combined possibilities of #2 [fifth position] and #3 [seventh position], plus a lot more that can't be done in either #2 or #3. This is because in #1 [sixth position], every other note has two fingerings/locations, except for the lowest and highest notes (low A; High D). Hammer-ons and pull-offs over a perfect 4th interval are now possible.

Note Math/Finger Math

Note Math

+=ascending

- =descending

1 + + + +
2 - - - -
3 + + + -
4 - - - +
5 + + - +
6 - - + -
7 + - + +
8 - + - -
9 - + + +
10 + - - -
11 + - + -
12 - + - +
13 + - - +
14 - + + -
15 + + - -
16 - - + +

Finger Math

1234	4321	1324	4231	1342	2431
2341	3214	3241	2314	3421	4312
3412	2143	2413	3142	4213	3124
4123	1432	4132	1423	2134	1243

24 X 4 (finger-stretch sequences) = 96 patterns.
(See Page 27)

Observations

Note Math:

- You could construct two measure patterns by starting on the note G. This would make 256 two-measure patterns (16 x 16). Example:

7 + - + +
14 - + + -
From C
From G

- You could play these patterns on all seven-note scales and modes.
- You could rewrite the whole series of 16 one-measure examples using other intervals besides 3rds (4ths, 5ths, 6ths, etc.).
- You could make a living by writing books of exercises using this material!

Finger Math:

- These 96 patterns could be played on one string, or in positions (across all six strings).
- You could construct chords and/or arpeggios by putting each of the four fingers on four different strings.
- You could take any group of four different notes (melody or arpeggio) and re-arrange it for 23 variations.
- Study the relationship between the 24 patterns (of Finger Math) and the material in "Fragments (Mosaics)."
- You could keep in mind that all of these are "possibilities"; they are not necessarily "music."

Fragments (Mosaics)

What follows is a compressed version of some material I came up with a long time ago. It all began with four notes: F F# G Ab. There are 24 possible arrangements of four notes (4 x 3 x 2 = 24). I constructed lines by connecting each of the 24 four-note patterns in descending minor 3rds. (Consequently most, if not all, of this material works nicely on a symmetrical diminished scale.) Then, I arrived at three other variations of the 24 lines by omitting the first note, the first two notes and the first three notes of the first measure. That makes 96 possibilities. The first measure of each of the 96 lines follows. If you want to reconstruct each line (or some lines), all you have to do is repeat whichever four note pattern you're using in descending minor 3rds. (If possible, try to play these without writing them out.)

Also, realize that these four- note patterns could be connected at *other* intervals besides minor 3rds. Not only that, but you could move from *any* four-note pattern to any other four-note pattern at any interval, ascending or descending! Obviously, these kinds of patterns are highly chromatic and probably won't sound too good against "Happy Birthday" or "Ave Maria"!

However, you might be able to find uses for some of them in certain kinds of contemporary improvised music. And one more thing: if the original four notes are changed to F F# G A, then all the 96 four note patterns would be different!

Fragments (Mosaics)

A 1
A 2
A 3
A 4
B 1
B 2
B 3
B 4
C 1
C 2
C 3
C 4

D 1
D 2
D 3
D 4
E 1
E 2
E 3
E 4
F 1
F 2
F 3
F 4

Voicings From The Symmetrical Diminished Scale

G Symmetrical Diminished (or Bb or C# or E)

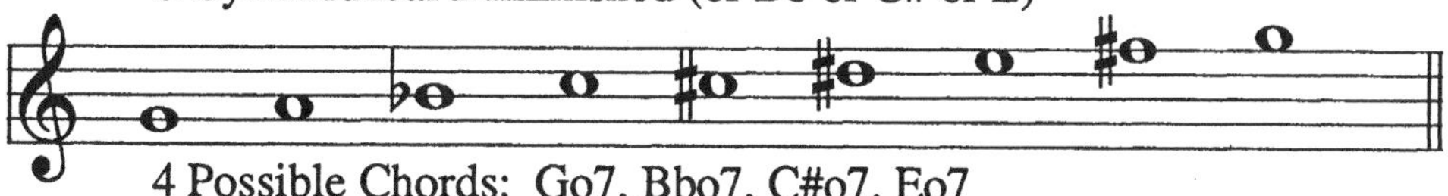

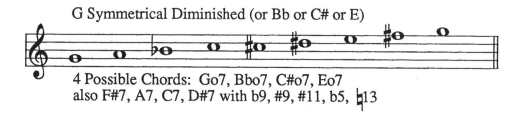

4 Possible Chords: Go7, Bbo7, C#o7, Eo7
also F#7, A7, C7, D#7 with b9, #9, #11, b5, ♮13

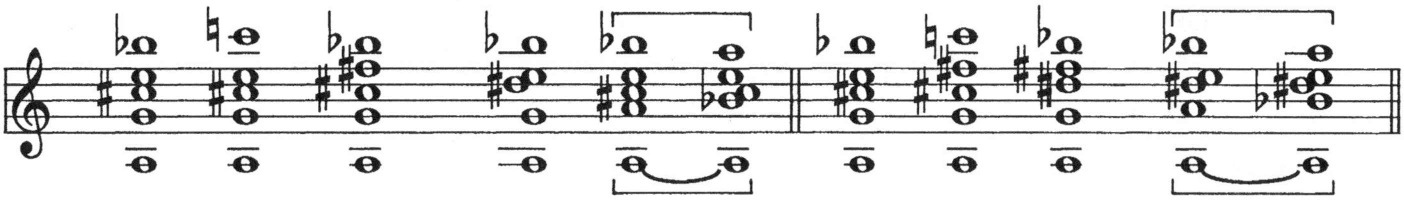

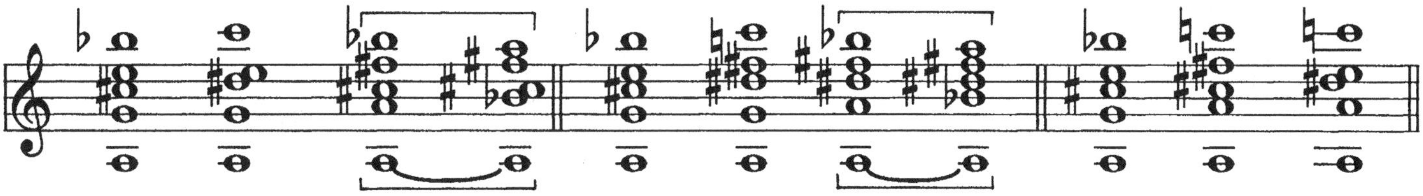

What do the bracketed groups all have in common?

Remember: all these voicings can be moved up or down in minor 3rds!

Symmetrical Diminished Scale

D# A- F# C- A D#- C F#-

Gb C- A D#-7 C F#- D# A-

D#- C F#- D# A- F# C- A

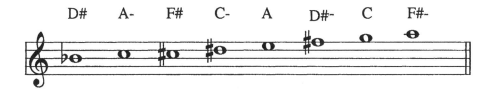

There are four major and four minor triads in the diminished scale:
A, A-, C, C-, D#, D#-, F#, F#-

1. Can you harmonize the scale three ways with closed triads?
2. Can you harmonize the scale three ways with spread triads?
3. Could those triads go over other bass notes from the scale?
4. Since all this material also works for C7, D#7, and F#7, how many different chords could you resolve to?
5. Since the diminished scale doesn't have any convenient "handles" on it (major, melodic minor, and harmonic minor scales do have "handles"!), aren't you glad that there are only three symmetrical diminished scales?
6. Is the altered dominant scale suddenly becoming much easier to use?

A Picture is Worth a Thousand Words — a Taste, a Thousand Pictures.

1. Play this:

2. Can you skip around from any one of the 16 measures to any other?
3. Is this theme based on a scale or part of a scale?
4. What chords could this theme work against?
5. Can you transpose this theme to any other mode? All other modes?
6. Can you memorize this theme and play with eyes closed?
7. Can you transpose this theme and play with your eyes closed?
8. If you can read this line, then your eyes aren't closed!
9. Can you play each measure backwards?
10. Can you play the whole theme backwards?
11. What would happen if you repeated any one of the notes?
12. What would happen if you started the theme in another place?
13. If you've gotten this far, what do you need with me any more?
14. Look at the title again. Do you understand why that's the title?

III. COMMENTARIES

The Guitar's Complexity

A long time ago, I made a chart that contained every note on the guitar, and showed every location and every practical fingering. (An example of an "unpractical" fingering would be to play Low F with your 4th finger!) Instead of writing it out, let me tell you what I learned from it:

- The range of the guitar is about 45 half steps. (We're not including any harmonics in this analysis.)
- The very low notes and the very high notes on the guitar have only one location and not too many fingerings, but concert middle C, which is in the middle register of the instrument, has five locations and about 16 different fingerings!
- When you calculate all the numbers, it comes out this way: the average note on the guitar has 2.8 locations and 9.2 fingerings!
- It's important to understand how very complicated the guitar really is. Also, how vast are its possibilities. This way, we can cultivate patience and stop worrying because we think we aren't learning fast enough. (To really know the guitar *has* to take a lot of time. Why be in such a hurry?)
- The next time someone complains to you because your sight reading "isn't what it should be," you'll know exactly what to tell them!

The Evolution:

1. When you limit yourself to only one note, you are not playing melody, nor are you playing harmony; but you could quite easily be playing with all other elements of music.
2. Limit yourself to only two notes on one string.
3. Limit yourself to only three notes on one string.
4. Limit yourself to only two notes on two adjacent strings.
5. Limit yourself to only three or four notes on two adjacent strings.

Another View:

1. Play with one note (one string).
2. Play with two notes (one string).
3. Play with three notes (one string).
4. Play with two notes (two strings).
5. Play with three or four notes (two strings).

Contemporary Harmony

Let's face it: compared to any keyboard instrument, the guitar is a rather limited harmonic instrument. Still, there's a lot to the guitar harmonically; but you have to work very hard at it for quite a long time. In order to "hold your own" against modern piano players these days (in the harmonic sense), there are certain areas that you should really work with a lot. These areas would include:

- Anything and everything having to do with quarter harmony (fourth harmony).
- Triads over bass notes (sometimes called "slash chords").
- Structures from the symmetrical diminished scale.
- Structures with half steps included in them. (Sometimes these structures could involve voicings with open strings mixed in with fretted notes.)
- Structures with b9 intervals included in them.

Also, keep in mind that it's not just how many voicing you know; it's much more a question of how many uses you know for each voicing. It's important to be able to analyze any particular structure in all twelve keys in order to come up with as many uses as possible. (As you may have deduced by now, I've done that a lot in this volume.)

In order to develop an "ear" for contemporary harmony, you'd be wise to listen primarily to pianists . (Most guitarists are still decades behind pianists, harmonically speaking.) My personal opinion is that the full harmonic potential of the guitar can only be realized if you play finger-style. Short of that, "pick and fingers" would be the next logical choice. But regardless of whether you play finger-style, "pick and fingers" or just with a pick, harmony on the guitar is still in its infancy. There's much yet to be done and there's room for everyone. So what are you waiting for?

About Tuning and Tuners:

When electronic tuners first came out, I was (sort of) "against" them. After a while, I got one and discovered (to my surprise) how very useful they are. Now, I'm "for" them.

Even though you use a tuner, you can still have intonation problems if each string is not in tune with itself. That's why some guitars have bridges with moveable saddles for each string. (I hope your guitar has one!) You need to get a small screwdriver to adjust the saddles. (On some guitars, you might need a very small allen wrench.) You need to use the screwdriver! (That is, if you want to play in tune.) Also, if possible, get a set of fine tuners (similar to what violins have): they really come in handy. So, to review:

1. Tune-o-matic type bridges.
2. Screwdriver (or allen wrench)
3. Electronic tuner
4. Fine tuners

Harmonics and Overtone Influence

This topic is one of the most interesting aspects of the guitar. One might almost say that it constitutes another instrument entirely—one that is superimposed over the guitar. It would be good to keep in mind that the overtone series is entirely based on mathematical laws, and that some acquaintance with a good book on acoustics would be of great value.

Nodes are the points where a string is divided into equal parts: 1/2; 1/3; 1/4; 1/5; 1/6; 1/7; 1/8; 1/9; etc. The frequency of the resultant partial is inversely proportional to the division of the string length. (Half the string length twice the frequency.)

Dividing the string into two parts gives one node (12th fret). Dividing the string into three parts gives two nodes (7th and 19th frets). Dividing the string into four parts gives three nodes (5th, 12th and 24th frets). However, since one of the nodes (the 12th fret) has already been used for a lower harmonic, only the 5th and 24th frets would produce the proper frequency. This occurs with any division of the string into a number of parts that can be divided by a smaller number (i.e., 4 /2 ;6 /3 or 2; 8 /4 or 2; 10 /5, etc.). Consequently, divisions of five and seven produce the greatest number of functioning nodes, (4 and 6 respectfully). As a result, we can see that there are a great number of available nodes that produce a variety of different pitches with certain repetitions. All of this occurs on a single string. (Remember, we have six strings altogether, don't we?) Now, as if this isn't confusing enough, keep in mind that many nodes are located above the top frets of the fingerboard. This may not seem to be very important, but keep this point in mind with what follows.

There are two distinctly different uses of the overtone series: one positive, the other negative. In playing harmonics, we are employing the positive use; that is, a finger lightly touches a string at a node while we pluck the string with the pick or right-hand finger. This action causes all other partials above and below the frequency of the node to be eliminated, leaving the node frequency alone to ring. An example of the negative aspect would be if you plucked the string exactly at the node point. Then, the exact opposite would happen. The node frequency would be eliminated and the other partial frequencies would be reinforced! Therefore, whether you know it or not, your right hand is juggling partials much of the time! To explore this subject in depth will, if nothing else, explain why timbre varies with the placement of the right hand. I feel I must stop writing at this point; it's like explaining how to tie a necktie to someone over the phone.

Feeling "Stale"?

Things to try when you feel "stale" (about your playing or music):

- Play on the tunes that you are currently playing, but at least twice as slow. (And no double time!) This way, if you start to play any of your "pet licks" (or your "beef stew"), it will sound so bad to you that you'll probably stop right in the middle and quite possibly actually start to improvise, since, at the slower tempo, you'll have much more time (and space) to think/hear/feel other kinds of ideas.
- Ask yourself: "Is there anything really important in music that I've forgotten about?"
- Feed a loaf (or two) of bread to some pigeons, ducks, sea gulls, or other types of birds.
- Imagine a time or circumstance where you could *never play the guitar again.*
- Go for a long walk.
- Cry.
- Stop playing the guitar and/or listening to music for 1, 2, 3, 4, 5, 6, or 7 days.
- Stop playing the guitar, but listen to a lot of music for 1, 2, 3, 4, 5, 6 or 7 days.
- Change the strings on your guitar and polish it.
- Send your guitar "back to the factory" to either be retuned or recycled.

Silence is Golden

As players, we are all guilty (at least sometimes) of playing too much. (Sometimes it seems that the worse we think it sounds, the more notes we play in order to make up for it. Usually, things get even worse.) We need to remind ourselves (over and over again) that quite often, "less is more". We need to think: "Don't play ten notes when one will do." We need to ponder the meaning of the expression: "Notes are clever ways of getting from one silence to another."

There is nothing that is easier to play on the guitar than silence. (Many of you are probably doing exactly that right now!) But knowing when, how, why, and for what length of time we should play, silence is not as easy.

For purposes of demonstration, I've gone to the trouble of transcribing a number of examples of "the effective use of space." These examples come from solos of mine (that I'm especially fond of) on several gigs I've played in the Boston area over the last six months, which fortunately just happened to be captured on tape. Of course, you must develop your own unique way of using space, so these examples shouldn't be taken too literally. Still, I thought it might be useful to include them.

Examples of "Effective Use Of Space".

1.

2.

3.

4.

5.

6.

7.

8.

9.

9a.

Observations

- Just because something is funny, it doesn't mean that it's not important.
- Just because something is important, it doesn't mean that it's not funny.
- One of the few things worth taking seriously is humor.

On Being Self-Critical

Students tend to think that eventually, after they learn whatever it is that they think they need to know (or they can do whatever it is they think they need to be able to do), they won't feel insecure anymore. This thinking amounts to wishing that you didn't dislike your playing so much. It's fantasizing that things will gradually change for the better.

Well, as good as it sounds on paper, it seldom (if ever) happens. In fact, it tends to get worse. If you start off being critical, you tend to remain that way, and more than likely, along with everything else, your criticalness will improve. If you try to deny your criticalness, that messes you up, because it amounts to lying. If you become critical of your criticalness, it's the same thing removed one step. If you think, "I shouldn't be so critical of myself," you're into "what should be" instead of "what is." My experience has shown me that being into "what is" is infinitely superior to being into "what should be." However, it's not as easy. (We all seem to love to get lost in "what should be"!)

Being self-critical actually has a lot to be said for it. People who are self-critical tend to improve in music because they always seem to see so many things to work on. They tend not to get involved in overly developed egos. They tend to be much less critical of everyone else. Often, they are compassionate.

Being self-critical also seems to involve a lot of attention paid to detail. I think you can see that this sort of thing is very important in music. Of course, some people seem to go overboard in this direction. That's a tough path to go because too much attention paid to detail can be stiffling in music, especially improvised music. Other things are important, too. Sometimes these other things have nothing at all to do with paying attention to detail; in fact, they might even appear to be exactly the opposite of it. So, as often happens, the idea of balance emerges.

Words - Terms

Frequency   Pitch   Intonation   (Vibrato)

Amplitude   Volume   Dynamics   Duration   Length

Attack/Termination   Decay/Sustain

Timbre   Tone   Overtone influence

Tempo   Meter   Beat   Time   Rhythm

Movement

Dance

Articulation

Vibrato   Slurs   Hammer-ons   Pull-offs

Grace note   Trills   Ornaments   Slides

Bending   Dynamics   Phrasing

Sound   Rests

Notes

Silence

Change   Contrast

Melody/Harmony   Intervals   Counterpoint

Expression Marks   Touch   Feeling   Emotion

Form   Space   Context

Consonance   Dissonance

Observations

- I've listed some important words that occur in music and the guitar.
- The order is not important (although you can see some sensible relationships).
- Every time I look at this page I usually see something I hadn't thought about before. (Or I see a different angle to something I have thought about before.)
- It's very interesting to use simple combinations of a few of these words as a sort of "springboard" or point of departure for a free improvisation.
- Examples: Improvised piece based on slides and bending. Improvised piece based on dynamics and silence. Improvised piece based on trills, vibrato, and contrast. Etc., etc...

No One Knows What's Next

There is a wonderful and very useful attitude toward improvising that can be cultivated. It is based on the realizations that:

- No one who is listening to you has any idea what you're going to play next.
- You don't have any idea what you're going to play next.

I would suggest that you look for these things at the end or completion of a melodic phrase. Maybe you'll begin to see why I make such a big deal out of silence. Also, you might figure out why some people never stop for very long! They don't want to realize these things. The first time a person becomes aware that "no one knows what's next," it can be pretty frightening. However, this realization can change into a truly amazing understanding. At first, it seems like the sting of a bee, but it can become sweet as honey later on.

After you've played a bit on a simple modal vamp, stop for a few seconds and ask yourself:

- What note will I play next?
- Will it be a short or long note?
- Loud or soft?
- When will I play it?
- Will it be followed by other notes?
- What kind of tone quality will it have?
- What am I trying to convey by this note?
- Is what I'm going to play similar to or different from what I've just played?
- Am I going somewhere with this note or am I arriving from somewhere with this note, or is it just there by itself?

Improvising Short Pieces (Use of the Tape Recorder)

Here's a useful project that you can do. Get a blank 60-minute cassette tape. Starting at the beginning of the tape, make a recording of yourself improvising a short piece (no longer than two minutes). When you've finished, turn off the tape recorder. Do not listen to the piece! On the following day, listen to the first piece, then record another one on the end of the first one. Do not listen to the new piece. On the third day, listen to the second piece and record a third one. Continue this procedure until both sides of the tape are filled with these short pieces. (This process should take about a month. You'll have about 30 2-minute improvisations.) Never listen to what you've recorded until the following day. This way, each piece will sound fresh since you'll have forgotten what you played.

When the tape is completely filled, set aside a couple of hours to listen to all of the pieces in succession. Hopefully, out of 30 two-minute improvisations, there should be at least a few of them that will obviously be better than the others. These pieces, or parts of them, can be used as ideas for compositions or tunes. In addition to these benefits, you will also be able to learn a lot about how you play. You might notice certain things in your playing by listening to yourself for a solid hour that you hadn't noticed before. For instance, you might catch yourself nodding off after about 15 or 20 minutes, and it might occur to you that the pieces lack dynamic contrast, for example. Or perhaps you might see that you tended to favor certain modes, tonalities, or rhythms to the exclusion of others. You could quite possibly learn a lot from such a project, in one direction or another. So, why not try it?

One of the most interesting uses of the cassette tape recorder is as an ear-training device. Here are some suggestions:

a. Play random notes from any scale or arpeggio, with a short pause between each note. While playing the tape back, try to duplicate each note during the pauses.

b. Strum any chord for four slow beats, switch to any other chord for four slow beats, then another, etc. Try to keep the chords completely unrelated, i.e., C, F#-, D7, D-7(b5), E7 alt., DbM7, etc.

While playing the tape back, try to improvise a simple melody (perhaps on one string) with one or two melody notes for each chord. This may be tricky at first, but eventually a person could develop this to an almost unbelievable extent.

Once I had a student who became so good at playing against unrelated chords in this fashion that he never made a mistake. I tried to confuse him with the weirdest voicings and progressions that I could think of, all to no avail. Then one day, in the middle of a long series of upper-structure triads over bass notes alternating with altered dominant 4th voicings over both the tritone and major 7th in the bass, I played a G7 going to C. The student stopped playing, looked at me in astonishment, and shouted, "What the @@!!@!!! was that?!"

Remember: almost any chord supports at least a six-note scale. Since there are only twelve notes, your chances of hitting a right note by luck are 50-50. And when you do hit a wrong note, (assuming you can discern a wrong note!), all you have to do to correct it is to move it up or down a half step.

c. Prerecord a melody; then try to improvise chords to it! (I wouldn't recommend trying this too much until you're pretty good at suggestion b.)

Time-Rhythm

I. Use a metronome. (It's a fantastic tool!) Be sure to play things at *all* settings available on the metronome. Don't just have three tempos: ballad, medium, as fast as possible. Use all the tempos. (There are certain things about "time" that you can't get into until you've "got the complete set.")

Learn to play three "styles" of time:

1. dead center
2. a bit ahead
3. a bit behind

Learning to play these three "styles" of time has to do with "placement." The sound and effect of a particular passage can be very different depending on where it's "placed" (center, ahead, behind).

Learn to use accents. It's very important. Accents give "life" and "definition" to music. (Keep in mind that slurring has accents "built in.")

Experiment with different ratios of "even notes to odd notes." For instance, "swinging" has traditionally been equated with a 2 to 1 ratio:

1st note	2nd note	3rd note	4th note
2	1	2	1
66.3 %	33.3 %	66.3 %	33.3%

In its most obvious form, 2 to 1 is a "shuffle feel". As far as "swing" goes, this is okay up to a point. Tempo affects it a lot. At medium-up to very fast tempos, 2 to 1 starts sounding "stiff" and eventually becomes impossible. Jazz 8th notes tend to become even 8th notes. Sometimes, if the off-beat notes are accented, the "swinging" feeling can be retained.

It would be useful to become familiar with the following ratios:

Obviously important:

50% - 50% (even 8ths)

2 1
66. 3% - 33. 3% (swing 8th; shuffle)

75% - 25% ()

25% - 75% ()

1 2
33. 3% - 66. 3% (inverse shuffle)

Useful

55% - 45% (jazz 8th variation)

60% - 40% (jazz 8th variation)

To review: three important considerations:

- placement (center, ahead, behind)
- accents (even or odd numbered notes)
- ratios of even to odd numbered notes

The combinations are infinite.

II. Rhythmical groupings: let's take the numbers 1 through 8. We all know 1, 2, 3, 4, 6, and 8 note groupings. Most of us are much less familiar with 5 and 7 note groupings. They are really very fascinating, once you get used to them.

(To digress for just a moment: take the numbers 1, 2, and 3; all other numbers can be arrived at by combining 1, 2, and 3.)

The 5's and 7's are very interesting because of the ways they "permute". (It's also interesting to realize how important 5 and 7 note scales are in music!

Learning how to use 5's and 7's is the beginning of "odd-meter" playing. There are two distinctly different ways of using them: firstly, they can be superimposed over other, more familiar, groupings:

5	5	5	5	5	5	
1	2	3	4	6	8	etc.

7	7	7	7	7	7	
1	2	3	4	6	8	etc.

Secondly, they can be grouped using common rhythmical units.

- 8th notes grouped in 5's or 7's
- triplets grouped in 5's or 7's
- 16th notes grouped in 5's or 7's

At this point, I wouldn't be surprised if you find that you've discovered some "virgin woods" for yourself. (I sure hope so!)

Not all musicians play chords. Not all musicians play melodies. But *all* musicians play rhythms. Drummers specialize in rhythms and time. Talk to them. Listen to what they play. (In the last five years, I've acquired only two books that pertain to music. Both of them were written by drummers!)

Hint: If you were to play the guitar in such a way as to eliminate harmony, melody, and even pitch, you'd be left with muffled strings. Suddenly, you're a drummer!

Tuning into "Time Headquarters": (A Mental, Emotional, and Verbal Improvisation)

Do you have a metronome?

A. Yes (Great!)

B. No (You'd better get one!)

How many tempos are there on your metronome? What is an "octave of time"? Is this like an octave in pitch? Does it follow from this, that when we play music, we are manipulating factors that come from different levels of vibrational ranges superimposed over each other or contained within each other, or co-existing with each other? Is there an easier way to say this? How about:

> Can a galaxy contain a solar system containing a planet, one hemisphere of which contains a continent in which a country contains a state, a particular city of which contains a street on which there is a building having a particular apartment (on a particular floor) in which there is a room containing a wet sponge saturated with coffee, which, in turn, is saturated with honey made up of certain molecules containing atoms containing electrons and so on into the night..."?

Is that an easier way to say it, or isn't it? How would you say it? Have we gotten sidetracked? Maybe so! But it was fun! (Have you ever heard the Bach Chaccone?)

I know an excellent bass player who, at one point anyway, was in the habit of coming home after a gig (perhaps having imbibed some beverage of one sort or another), sinking into his favorite chair and turning on his T.V. to watch bowling (with the sound turned off) while simultaneously listening to his metronome click at one of his favorite tempos. (Say MM = 160) Why do you think he would do that? What do you think he learned from that?

How would a person find out?

Is there such a place as "Time Headquarters"? Is there a device for tuning into this place? If one tunes into this place, what is one tuning into? How much music can exist at mm = 100? At any tempo? At all tempos? (Did you just spill your coffee? Do you have a sponge?)

Some people have said that if you play with a metronome your "time will get stiff." I wonder about that statement. Is it possible that some people "project"? (You know, putting things inside them outside of themselves or seeing things that way...) I think it is possible; we all do it.

I've known many people who work with metronomes who don't sound stiff to me. (But maybe I'm projecting! Could be. But what am I projecting?) Maybe if "beauty is in the eye of the beholder," then "stiffness" is in the ear of the listener, or "swing" is in the ear of the listener. (Or anything else, for that matter.)

Say these words to yourself. Think about them. How does each word make you feel?

		Write your own:
1. Groove	6. Cookin'	10.
2. Swing	7. Smokin'	11.
3. "In the pocket"	8. Locked in	12.
4. Poppin'	9. Elbows and knees	13.
5. Edge		

Now say the words again while listening to a metronome.

I think a metronome is as good as the person using it. If we can learn to use it to tune into "Time Headquarters", we can learn much. The infinitely perfectable experiences of regularly recurring periodicity. (Certainly, there's a better way to say that!) (Have you ever heard the Bach Chaccone?)

If a tree falls in a forest and there's no one to hear it, does it make a sound? (Or land on top of anyone, for that matter?)

If a metronome clicks in the forest and there's no one to hear it, does it swing?

(I once saw a squirrel carrying a miniature soprano sax...)

Beware of beavers bearing baritones,
but promote peacocks practicing pianos and
trust turkeys tooting tenors.

Near miss #1: Love vegetables, don't eat them.
Near miss #2: The girl next door.

"It's just the Near Miss of Yew."
"It's just the meer-ness of you."
"It's just the mirror-ness of you."

Tempo-Movement

Pick a tempo you want to work with. Find it on your metronome. While the metronome is ticking, start some activity that will take between 5-15 minutes to complete. (Washing dishes, preparing food, cleaning up a messy desk, shaving, watering plants, whatever...) While doing this activity (and listening to the metronome), try to observe all of your movements relative to the tempo of the metronome. Experiment with changing the speed of your movements to synchoronize with the metronome. (Generally speaking, it's advisable to experiment this way with slower rates of movement. Later on, however, you might want to try speeding up the rate of movement.)

After the task is completed, turn off the metronome. Sit quietly for a couple of minutes. Notice what your mind is doing...

Turn the metronome on again (same tempo). Pick up a guitar and start playing something with the metronome. (Improvise on a mode, play on a tune, whatever...) After enough time (you must be the judge of that!), put down the guitar. Turn off the metronome. Sit quietly again for a couple of minutes.... Pick up the guitar again. *Without* the metronome, try to play at the same tempo as well as you can remember. After a short time, turn on the metronome to check whether the tempos are the same or not. If not the same, make a mental note of whether you slowed down or sped up.

Leaving the metronome ticking, put down the guitar.

Stand up in an area where you have sufficient room to move around. Start moving your arms in small, slow circles to the metronome.

Experiment: four- measure circles, two- measure circles, one-measure circles,etc., etc. Move your head in similar ways. Then move your legs (probably one at a time!) Try other parts of the body: shoulders, elbows, knees, hands, feet, hips, etc. Rest as often and as long (or short) as necessary. This exercise is not supposed to be aerobic dancing. Move much slower. It's more like Tai-chi or ballet. Don't be concerned with doing it "well." Do it more for fun. Think "movement," not "exercise." Pay a lot of attention to the quality of movement. Especially to how it feels. Try to move in ways that feel good.

When you're finished, turn off the metronome. Sit quietly again for 5-10 minutes. Notice what your mind is doing....

Afterthoughts

- There are a lot of different tempos that you could work with this way.
- This approach tends to get tempos into your whole system in a very deep and organic way.
- You can learn a great deal about attention through doing this sort of thing.
- Movement, attention, thinking, feeling, and breathing are all connected.
- You might enjoy trying this again later on using music (record, tape, radio) instead of the metronome.
- You could try it again without using either music or the metronome.

Some Thoughts on Technique

Usually, when we think of guitarists as having "great technique," what we mean is: how fast they play; how clean (precise) they play. But technique really involves much more than that. It also involves how slow; how sloppy; and everything else in between all of these extremes. Technique is touch. It's also movement. It's the point where *what's inside you* (intention, thought, feeling, etc.) meets the instrument and is transformed into what's outside you (sound, music). For a guitarist, this means primarily hands and fingers (also wrists, arms, shoulders, neck, and back, but in a less obvious way). Technique includes everything involved in the way(s) you play the instrument physically. (Whenever you play anything on the guitar, technique is involved.)

One of the most important things to keep in mind relative to technique is what I call "efficiency of energy expenditure." This phrase means to use exactly the right amount of energy for whatever the task at hand requires — no more and no less. (Think of focusing a lens on a movie projector; there's really only one very small area where the image is in clear focus. Good technique is like that.) The other thing that needs to be considered is the coordinated balance of the two hands. Now, every guitarist who can play even a little does have a coordinated balance between the two hands already. However, it may not necessarily be the most efficient balance that could be possible in terms of energy expended. Sometimes this is very difficult for people to see in themselves for two reasons. Firstly, you are already used to the "feel" of whatever kind of balance your hands are accustomed to, so you don't tend to think of other possibilities of balance between your hands. Secondly, a lot of inefficient energy expenditure is very "hidden." (So "hidden," in fact, that you have to be pretty clever and very observant in order to find it at all!)

Let's see if we can clarify this point.

Suppose you want to play the A on the 5th fret of the high E string. You decide what finger (left hand) you're going to use. You place it right below the 5th fret (very close to the fret). Then you pluck the string with a pick or a right-hand finger (or thumb). One of two things happens: either the note rings out clear, or else it doesn't ring out clear. Right? If it *doesn't* ring clear, we all know that more energy is needed in the left-hand finger. If it does ring clear, we'd tend to think everything is just fine. Right? Okay, now let's look at what's "hidden." The first thing that's "hidden" is that when the note doesn't ring clear, it could ring clear if the right hand picks the string at a lower volume level. So a more complete assessment of the situation that occurs when the note doesn't ring clear would be: Either too little energy in the left-hand finger, *or* too much energy in the right hand. The second thing that's "hidden" is that when the note does ring clear, you might be using more energy in the left-hand finger than is necessary. (How can you tell? The note is clear, so you think "Mission Accomplished"!) So, a more complete assessment of the situation that occurs when the note does ring clear would be: *Either* too much energy in the left-hand finger, *or* too little energy in the right hand. (Either you're wasting energy in the left-hand for the volume the right hand is playing, or else you're not attacking the string hard enough given the energy level of the left hand finger.) Often, we tend to blame one hand when we'd be much better off examining the balance between both hands.

Most of us use far too much energy in our left hand. This kind of energy waste is very "hidden." We don't want notes to buzz, so we overcompensate with too much left-hand energy. (Once you start to examine this in detail, you may begin to notice unevenness between the four left-hand fingers. Many guitarists use more energy with the "little" finger than with the other three fingers. Again, a case of overcompensation.)

So, what can we do about all of this? Well, there are a number of different things to try:

1. Play a note over and over at a regular and even rate (maybe quarter notes at MM = 80) and at the same volume level. Experiment with left-hand finger by gradually relaxing the pressure until the note begins to buzz a little. Continue lessening the pressure until the note actually ceases to be a clear pitch at all and is just a muffled attack with no sustain. Then gradually increase the pressure back through all the "buzz" stages until the note rings clear again. Even after it's clear, keep adding

pressure so you can see and understand what was explained before about the "hidden" waste of energy. Then start to relax the pressure again until you reach the buzz point. "Hang out" at the buzz point for a while. Go back and forth between clear note and very slight buzz. (This is the area where the projector is in focus.)

2. Go through the same procedure again, but this time reverse the ways the hands are working. This means that the left-hand pressure stays exactly the same while the right-hand pressure changes to produce buzzes. Clear notes will occur at lower volume levels, while buzzes and "muffled un-notes" occur at higher volume levels. (I guess we could call these two exercises: "Never letting either hand know what the other is doing"! It's also another example of "keeping one thing the same while the other changes, and changing one thing while the other stays the same.")

3. Here's an interesting idea: when you play melodies, you're playing one note at a time. Experiment with using the fingers of the left hand in such a way that you never have more than one finger on the fingerboard at a time. This means that the other three fingers that are not involved in playing the note are always "in the air" and free to move anywhere at any time. This also means that you have to lift each previous finger at the same moment that each new finger decends to fret the next note. (Tip: play long passages of very slow notes as legato as possible: no spaces at all between the notes.)

   As interesting as this idea is, don't think that you have to play this way all the time. It's just that you could learn a lot by experimenting with it, and you might find that it's very useful for some kinds of playing.

4. Play the guitar without using the right hand at all! All notes will be sounded by left-hand fingers falling on the frets. This is an especially good way to determine exactly which fingers tend to "overcompensate," because you'll hear those notes accented.

All of these exercises are a bit difficult at first. Because of the fact that everyone already has a habitual (but not necessarily efficient) balance between the two hands, you'll see that it's difficult to keep one hand the same while the other changes. (Interestingly enough, this difficulty is actually the evidence that there is a balance.)

This means that what you're really doing with these exercises is destroying the values of pressures and balances that you programmed into your hands while you were first learning to play the instrument. Don't be surprised if you feel uncomfortable at first. (Sometimes bad habits "die hard.") But if you understand what you're doing and why you're doing it (in terms of re-education and/or reprogramming), there should be no serious problem. In fact, it could very easily be *more* than worth the effort involved.

Different Playing Situations

As musicians, we find ourselves in different playing situations all the time. These different situations usually fall into one of three categories:

1. Playing alone
2. Playing with other musicians
3. Playing with other musicians for an audience.

What everyone would like is to be able to play well all of the time. Unfortunately, "wishing does not make it so". Everyone would like to be able to play with"consistency." My experience has shown me that consistency usually only appears after you've given up all hope of ever achieving it.

I used to wonder (about 12 years ago) why it was that I could only play certain kinds of things by myself at 2:00 in the morning in my apartment. It seemed that I could never play these kinds of things on gigs or at sessions. It really puzzled me.

After about four years, I wondered why it was that I could only play certain kinds of things with other musicians for large audiences. It seemed that I could never play these kinds of things at sessions or by myself. It really puzzled me.

Then it finally occurred to me that (all along) I'd been expecting certain things of myself regardless of the playing situation. I realized how unrealistic these expectations were, and how they were actually undermining my ability (in a subtle way) to respond spontaneously in different situations.

About that time, I completely abandoned any hope of playing consistently. I realized that every time I played (regardless of the situation), it was "the first and last in a series of One." Not surprisingly, my playing started to become somewhat more consistent all by itself. By then, I wasn't even concerned with consistency anymore. I'd actually become more interested in "being in the moment" as much as I possibly could. (This seems very important, especially with regards to improvisation.)

To expect yourself to play well all of the time is silly. To be unaware of the differences involved in the three kinds of playing situations is to be unrealistic. (This is not to say that it's wrong to want to play well, to try to play as well as you can. These things are perfectly natural. It's just the unrealistic expectations that are a problem.)

There are very real differences between playing by yourself, playing with others, and playing with others for others in terms of necessity and available energies of different kinds. If you're always looking for the same results, you're probably too busy to actually see what's going on in any particular situation. The way I finally formulated it all for myself:

"A concert in Dayton on April 12, 1975 only happens once!"

While I'm on the subject, one other kind of playing situation needs to be considered: recording. Recording (especially in a recording studio) is a pretty weird thing from certain standpoints. Recording would seem to fall into category three, (playing with other musicians for an audience), except for the fact that the "audience" is not there while you play. The "audience" is potentially quite large, stretched out in time for who-knows-how long. When the "audience" is there, (hearing the record), you are *not* there. (But the music is.) There seems to be some sort of strange "time-travel in both directions" going on with recording. It's especially weird when you're recording improvised music, because your're dealing with two contrary attitudes:

Attitude A:

Relax
Have a good time
Be spontaneous
Allow yourself to be creative
Be in the moment; go with the flow
Etc., etc....

Attitude B:

What you play will always stay the same.
Anyone who wanted to could listen to what you played many times.
Critics could review the recording!
Don't play anything you might regret at any time in the future.
Do you have any idea how much it costs just to turn on this 24-track?
Etc., etc....

Recording is probably the most difficult thing to do. Recording music can be viewed as a way to "kill" music. Actually, maybe "freezing" would be more realistic. It's a lot like putting a bird in a cage. (You've always got the bird to look at, but you'll never see it fly or hunt for worms and insects!)

Recording is like going for a walk on the beach and then turning around to see the footptints you left behind. I think it's useful to realize that, within the whole history of music on this planet, recording is a very recent development. It has obviously changed the nature of music already and will continue to do so in the future.

Believe me, I'm not trying to say that recording is a bad thing. For every problem recording presents, it also provides a distinct advantage. (Maybe two, even!) Recording is *both* good and bad. However, I think it's very important for musicians to think about these things often. To ponder them.

Playing vs. Improvising

Even though a lot of us are "improvisers," we spend a large percentage of time "playing" things that we know. We mix it up a lot, to be sure, but most of it involves things that we've worked with (to one extent or another) and things that we are (at least somewhat) familiar with.

"Pure" improvising is different than "playing." "Pure" improvising involves things that are *unknown;* things that you've *never* played before; things that you are *unfamiliar* with. "Pure" improvising is exhaustingly hard work. If it happens to you even a few times a year, you should consider yourself fortunate. (However, it might be useful to keep in mind that "pure" improvising is sometimes experienced subjectively as being *anything* but a lot of fun. Sometimes it can be very confusing. Sometimes, even painful. On the other hand, sometimes it can be incredibly sublime and satisfying.)

"Playing" real well can happen a lot more often than "pure" improvising. Really great players seem to have the ability to consistently "slip into" some moments of "fairly pure improvising" and mix these moments with their "known playing vocabulary" in such a way that most of the people who listen to it would feel that they're listening to "pure" improvising. This is a very valuable skill to cultivate (to whatever extent you *can* cultivate it).

You can't force "pure" improvising. It's just something that can "happen". But even though you *can't* "make it happen," you *can* prepare yourself for when it *does* happen.

Selected Short Subjects

- Competition: If compete you must, try to keep it to yourself.
- The faster you play, the further ahead you have to look (and/or hear).
- Control usually involves slowing down.
- No single approach seems to work all the time.
- Practice has to do with preparing yourself for real music.
- A lot of comping has to do with seeing larger forms.
- Try using vu meters when working with dynamics.
- Remember: music is (basically) a communal sport.
- Listen to how the audience listens (whether it's one person or 10,000).
- Don't neglect your musical roots.
- Are you totally responsible for what you play? Of course not.
- To keep learning: aim at always being a beginner.
- Listen to the music that you play. It will tell you things.
- One of the few things that's worth taking seriously is humor.
- The one activity that you learn the most from is playing.
- All the material that you accumulate for one tonality can become available in many other tonalities (if you work at it!).
- There have been (and still are) many great guitarists. Listen to them.
- If even one person listens to you, your playing is drastically altered.
- About tempos:
  If it feels fast, feel it in half time.
  If it feels slow, feel it in double time.
- My own personal hope for this book is that it will be useful not so much for what's in it, but rather for what it points to.
- Students often ask me: "Should I do A or should I do B?" Most of the time, I ask them: "Why not do both?"
- Sometimes, when you see something vast, don't try to go after the whole thing; just take a bite out of it for a start.
- It's very important to be able to find the appropriate emotional energy for whatever is being played.
- *Comp*ing means to ac*comp*any. Hopefully, it also means to *comp*liment (and to support).
- Person working on "time" with a metronome: "An imperfect version of perfection." Also, "A perfect version of imperfection."
- Solo on a tune with changes and limit yourself to one octave (low, middle, or high register).

- **Dynamics:** Find the middle. This is important because you can either go up or down from there.

- The very best thing I (as the author) could say about this book is that I wish someone had written it 25 years ago.

- You are there because the audience is. (Hopefully) The audience is there because you are. (Hopefully)

- Remember: if it sounds good and/or feels good, you must be doing something right.

- No one is better at exactly what you're doing than you. Also, no one is worse at it.

- No matter how good you get, there's more. Go after it, improve it, play it, and give it away. Never try to be the best. Always try to be the best that you can be.

- What you could learn from playing with a metronome is "continuity". (What good rhythm sections specialize in is "continuity!')

- It's never too late to learn something new (or too soon). You're never too old to improve an area of your playing (or too young).

- It seems that the better you get, the more you see the importance of "fundamentals."

- In music, your greatest sense of identity usually occurs when "you" are hardly there at all.

    OR

  What we're all looking for is probably closer to nothing than to something.

- Don't ever forget: when you're playing music, someone is listening.

- Sometimes it's better to be aware of the intentionality rather than the specifics.

- One of the things you have to do is forget all of this and just play music.

- Music comes from life. Many times you'll find that you learn more about music from life than from music.

- If you truly love what you're doing, you can handle failure or you can handle success. (In fact, I would think that's the only way anyone could handle success.)

- When it comes right down to it, we probably don't really know very much about how it is that we learn; but we know that we can learn. (Do we really need to know *how* we learn?)

- All playing requires energy.
  Good playing requires attention.
  Great playing requires passion (and maybe some luck, too!).

- No matter what level you're at, there is always:
  "Okay, let's cut out the "beef stew" for a while and see what we really mean!"
  (To play).

- Don't try to make a study of your own individuality. (That's what each person's whole life amounts to anyway!) Make studies of everyone else's individuality.

- Diminished scales are tricky because they don't have a convenient "handle" on them like the major, melodic minor, and harmonic minor scales do. Fortunately, there are only three diminished scales.

- It's not how many modes you know, or voicings for chords, or technical ability that matters. What matters is what you *do* with those things.

- Often, we forget that no one who's listening has any idea of what we might play next. (A good time to try to remember this is at the end of phrases; that is, when we aren't playing anything.)

- On "Free Playing": Sometimes it's helpful to think less about note choice and more about other considerations (tone, shape, color, dynamics, emotions, etc.).

- All purpose expression: Whenever you see *anything* (inside yourself or outside yourself) say, "Whatever it is, it's an absolutely perfect example of whatever it is!"

- Don't be afraid to look at the musicians that you are playing with. Don't be afraid to look at the people you're playing to. And even if you are afraid, look anyhow. You'll learn much.

- Everyone may not have the ability to become a great guitarist; but everyone does have the ability to improve, to get better. To me, that's more important.

- Sometimes if you close your eyes while you're playing, you can hear better.
  Sometimes if you look around while you're playing, you can gather energy
  (or exchange it).

- From one standpoint, no one knows your playing better than you (and never will)!
  From another standpoint, everyone else knows your playing better than you (and always will)!

- Learn to play the guitar with just your left hand.
  Learn to play the guitar with just your right hand.
  Learn to play the guitar with both hands.
  Learn to play the guitar with neither.

- "Notes are clever ways of getting from one silence to another."
  To what extent can silence help to portray sound?

  To what extent can sound help to portray silence?
  (Can you "play" silence?)

- The music that you play is for *other people*.
  (The music that other people play is for you.)
  But...
  the "playing" of the music that you play is for *you*.

- Sensitivity can never become automatic. The "trappings" of sensitivity can become automatic, but that's something else. By its very nature, sensitivity is diametrically opposed to anything automatic.

- Could a person's whole approach to learning how to improvise be improvised?
  How about half of it? (Exactly 50%!)
  How about roughly __________%? (fill in)

- One difference between practicing and playing is that when you practice, you pay a lot of attention to mistakes. When you play, you either ignore mistakes or else you "recover" from them (which is to *use* them).

- The most difficult thing about finding "your own path" is that you're *already on it* (whether you like it or not)! More than likely (whether you know it or not), you've *never left it!* That's why *finding* it is so difficult.

- Working with dynamics: Establish for yourself what soft, medium, and loud are. After that, proceed to rare, medium-rare, medium, medium-well, and well done. (And if you see the need for a "seven-speed dynamic transmission," who would know?)

- Playing "beyond yourself": When you play great for other people, (especially when it's *with* other musicians) it's a gift (for everyone!). Be thankful. Realize not so much that *you* did it, but rather that it must have been *needed* at the time (or at least, possible at the time).

- If you find that you're "nervous" when you play (especially for very large or very small audiences), accept it as being perfectly natural. *Don't* try to "make it stop." *Do* try to use this energy to play music. (Perhaps the energy needs "refining" to a certain extent; but don't ever think that this kind of energy is "bad" or "wrong." Perhaps you need to get used to it.)

- When you don't like the way you're playing:
  Try to change your attitude instead of changing the content.

  OR

  Try to like what you play instead of playing what you like.
  (To the extent that you can change your attitude, the content will take care of itself!)

- There are *many* ways to listen. Don't assume that just because you're a musician, you already know what it means to listen. Learning how to listen is an ongoing activity that you can improve. But only if you work at it. (Listening can be *incredibly powerful* in a subtle way.)

- Music is like life on a small scale,
  Life is like music on a large scale.

- If you ever get tired of the C scale,
  Just remember that
  The fool who persists in his folly shall someday
  B Locrian. (Natural, too!)

- Two kinds of playing:

  A. Playing on one chord (scale, mode)

  B. Playing through a progression of chords

  The first kind of playing is like making a curve go through a straight line. The second is like making a straight line go through a curve.

- Sometimes the elements of a person's unique style may be almost totally unknown as such. (They may be known, but if anything, disliked, because you think or wish that you should or could sound different than you do).

- Individuality seems to have a lot to do with being true to yourself. Being true to yourself is not always easy. In fact, you may have to teach yourself how to do it. Finding your own "voice" is not always pleasant. When your own "voice" emerges, you may not even recognize it.

- Picking and slurring: One way of playing the guitar involves attacking *every* note. (Similar to a pianist who *must* attack every note.) Another way of playing the guitar involves attacking *some* notes and slurring (hammer-ons and pull-offs) other notes. (Similar to a horn that can *either* attack or slur.) If at all possible, it's advisable to learn both ways of playing. Then you have it all!

- In thinking about dissonance and consonance, realize that there are two important considerations: (1) dissonance and consonance by *structure* and (2) dissonance and consonance by *function* (use). For example, a C major triad is a consonant structure. If it's used against a C chord or an A-7 chord, it's consonant in its *function*. If it's used for BbM7#11 or F#7 alt., it's dissonant by *function*.

- One thing that everybody has in common is pain. See if you can learn to play from your pain. Even if you don't think you're successful at it, or that it's doing any good, it may all come together for you one day. If that happens (even just one time), you'll find that the preparation was more than worth the effort because you might experience something that could change your understanding of music, people, and life in a very fundamental way.

- In music, many things are important: knowledge of the instrument; knowledge of the musical materials; technique; time; rhythm, phrasing; consonance and dissonance; tension and resolution; theme and variation; change; rest; sound; silence; dynamics; articulations; intention; feelings; ideas; movement; sensitivity; and luck to mention only a bunch. But if you had to pick *one* thing as being the *most* important, you'd probably have to choose "*hearing.*" (Beethoven not withstanding, how many great musicians have there been who were deaf?)

- Musical materials and the guitar are somewhat *inert*. A person's learning process is very *organic*. When we forget about our own learning process, we run into trouble. Sometimes we expect too much of ourselves. Music can become a very neurotic activity. When this happens, it's no use saying that it should be different than what it *is*. Don't think about what it should be. Look at what it is! When you see something very clearly, it practically changes by itself:

  Attitude A:
  Practicing even 8ths. "Those aren't even! That sounds terrible! I can't do it! Got to try harder! Maybe I don't have what it takes...?"

  Attitude B:
  Practicing even 8ths. "Those aren't even. Let me study very closely exactly how they aren't even. Hmmm! Very interesting...!"

- In studying this material, you might have a tendency to feel overwhelmed, like you could never possibly learn all this. If that happens, remind yourself that:

  1. You'd be amazed at what a human being could learn, given a lot of time.

  2. This material is not nearly as important as the music that it might be able to help you to play.

- Patience is so important. We can't help the fact that we usually want everything right now. However, experience usually teaches us at least not to expect it. Things unfold at their own pace; they take time. Just hang in there. Do what you see needs to be done. Work on what you see needs work. Make it as interesting as you can for yourself. Who cares how long it takes? Don't look for results. (If you work on what needs work, results will take care of themselves) Let them surprise you! Music is infinitely perfectable. It just takes a lot of work, a lot of time, and as much love as you can find.

In It, What's In It — No Regrets

Probably one of the most terrible feelings a human being can experience is regret. Especially the sort of regret that is not so much for what we did that was wrong, but rather for what we could have done (but didn't) that was right. The good thing about this feeling of regret is that, if we experience it often enough and deeply enough, we eventually see the importance of turning around our attitude and changing our life so that there would *never* be a reason for us to feel that way again in the future. If that happens, then regret has been useful to us. It has taught; we have learned. Regret consumes itself. (Many know the use of usefulness; few know the use of uselessness.)

Within a person's entire musical life, many different things will happen. Hopefully (and hopefully sooner, not later) you realize that any particular "period" of your musical life is unique, useful, and might possibly occur only once (at least in its present form). Suppose you're practicing a lot; working hard at it. This practicing period goes on for months, but you're not playing gigs (probably because there aren't any at that time or else no one's asking you). Naturally, you're going to reach a point (sooner or later) when you'll *really* want to play gigs. You might even begin to dislike practicing. Now let's say that, all of a sudden, you start to get some gigs. Feels good, right? Of course! But let's say further, that as time goes on, you keep getting more and more gigs until eventually, it seems that all you're doing is playing gigs. That could very possibly start to be a bit of a drag (for any number of different reasons). But let's say that while you were playing all these gigs you were beginning to see more and more clearly exactly what kinds of things you needed to work on (some of which you may not have even known existed before):

- Wow, I never realized how bad my time can be!
- I sure don't know enough voicings for minor 7(b5) chords...
- I need to learn more tunes!
- I need to work on my reading!
- Still can't cut those fast tempos.
- I don't like my sound.
- My comping is insensitive.
- My guitar is out of tune!
- What is a Maj. 7#5 chord, anyhow?
- I don't know the avoid note in the chromatic scale!
- Etc., etc....

Not surprisingly, at such times you would very naturally want to start working on "all the things you aren't!" (An incredible improvising guitarist: knows and plays all styles; has an enormous harmonic vocabulary in at least 23 different idioms; perfect time; exceptional chops; transposes all the Bach Violin Sonatas and Partitas up a tritone on sight; knows every tune ever written; is especially fond of 11/16, 5/4, and groups of 11 over 13 on a shuffle feel; has a reputation as a "computer destroyer" because three different brands of personal computers all exploded when this guitarist's solo on the Blues in Bb was fed into them to be analyzed; is such a sensitive accompanist that no woman vocalist who has worked with this guitarist has ever been able to sing more than 24 bars of any ballad without breaking into tears and sobs. Etc., etc.)

But assuming you're working all these gigs, you just don't have the time to practice as much as you would like. Suddenly, you remember back to the time when you were practicing a lot but not playing any gigs:

- Wow! I wish I had the chance to practice as much now as I did then!
  Boy, if I had only known then what I know that I don't know now, I would have done it a lot differently.

Now, let's say that suddenly (as if by magic), all the gigs stop (for any number of reasons). You've got all kinds of time to practice. Feels good! Right? Of course! So you work on what you see needs work (which is exactly what you should be doing!) But, eventually, you'll start wishing you had some gigs to play. Not only that, but you might begin to appreciate some things about all the gigs you did during your "gig period" that you didn't appreciate before:

- You know, that bass player was really a lot better than I realized. The time was so steady and firm. I was getting so bent out of shape in realizing how weak my own sense of time was compared to this bass player's that I never really listened to how good the time felt. Since this bass player has left town and moved to New York, who knows, I might never get a chance to play with this person again.
- (To which I would add: Who knows, you might not ever get a chance to play with *any other* bass player that good!)
- You know, I really learned so much from that piano player. I wish I could voice chords half as well as that person did. I probably should have asked more questions about harmony and voicings. Why didn't I?
- I sure do miss playing for people. It's so much easier to play well when someone is listening. But I was always so down on my own playing that I never really took advantage of the opportunity to communicate with people, to give.
- You know, that bartender really knew how to make a dry vodka martini!
- You know, that waitress really was cute!
- Etc., etc....

In walks "regret". Based on your current understanding of things, you come to see that you didn't realize the value of some previous period of your musical life or take advantage of it to the fullest extent. (In truth, you probably *did* do the best you could at the time, given the circumstances and your level of understanding, but the *feeling* afterwards is that you didn't.) The only way out of the dilemma of "perpetually regretting everything six months after the fact" is to realize that every period of your musical life, no matter how long or short, is very useful for some things, and that you need to be aware of what's useful (as well as what's useless) as much as you possibly can as much of the time as you possibly can. Let every situation that you experience be like "a good fire, that consumes all the fuel, leaving only dead ashes." Then, in every situation and/or period, you'll see "in it, what's in it, with no regrets."

Conclusion (read this again in one year)

Keep in mind that, as you continue to learn and improve, your understanding of all the material in this volume will change. What seems complicated at first gradually becomes easier and clearer. What seems "far-out" gradually becomes "nothing special." What you acquire as "skillful means" gradually becomes like "legs on a snake." Eventually (and to whatever extent you are capable of it), you become free of all this "material." You see that the problems that you have in music (and on the guitar) are clearly reflected in the problems that you have in life (and as a person).

It all becomes the same thing. You play. You live. You enter:

> *The Pathless Land, leaving no traces, no footprints.*
>
> *For long years a bird in cage,*
> *today, flying along with the clouds*
>
> — The Zenrin

Finally, and at long last, I have nothing more to say about this subject, whatever it was....